The Anatomy of Poverty

The Anatomy of Poverty

The Condition of the Working Class
in Montreal 1897-1929

Terry Copp

McClelland and Stewart Limited

for my parents

The Canadian Publishers
McClelland and Stewart Limited
25 Hollinger Road, Toronto

Printed and bound in Canada

Contents

The Canadian Social History Series   7
Preface   9
Acknowledgements   11

---

1   The City Below the Hill   15
2   The Real Incomes of the Working Class   30
3   Women and Children in the Labour Force   44
4   Formal Education and the Working Class   57
5   Housing Conditions   70
6   Public Health   88
7   Welfare   106
8   Labour Unrest and Industrial Conflict   128
9   Conclusion   140

Appendix A   149
Appendix B   164
Bibliographical Note   174
Notes   176
Index   188

Photograph Acknowledgements

From the Notman Photographic Archives,
McCord Museum of McGill University
-pages 16, 20, 24

From the Archives of the Montreal Urban
Community Transportation Commission
-pages 37, 78, 142

From the Public Archives of Canada
-page 46

From the Catalogue of the Child Welfare
Exhibition, Montreal 1912
-pages 72, 90, 98

The Canadian Social History Series

Social history is about people. This series is concerned with broadening the understanding of Canadian history, widening it from a story of past politics to a portrayal of the context in which Canadians have lived and interreacted with one another.

The series takes the broadest possible view of the subject matter of social history. It is concerned not only to encompass as much of the sweep of Canadian history as possible, but also to exploit the whole range of scholarship in this country. That means that it is interested in the social history of our native peoples, in immigration and acculturation, in the development of social institutions such as the family, classes, and voluntary organizations, in ideas and attitudes in their social context, in the social dimension of occupations and industries, in community formation and urban growth, in social movements such as the temperance crusade, the movement for prison reform, and that for the liberation of women, in sports and leisure activities. Social history is the history of the full range of human life, and this series will attempt to represent that range.

Canadian social history is still in its infancy. In few of the areas mentioned above has scholarship developed to the point at which a monograph covering any one of them for the whole time-span could be written. This series, therefore, proposes to take advantage of the work being done on specialized areas and fairly brief chronological periods. Without being narrow, the volumes will present in-depth studies of major themes, rather than sweeping generalities over the whole of Canadian history. Obviously it is hoped that, eventually, the series will build to a comprehensive social history of Canada; in the meantime, the individual volumes will be exemplary of both the subject matter and the approaches of that social history.

Our aim is a series which will be of use both to general readers and to students of history. All of those interested in the development of this country will find excitement in these studies of the major themes of social history. At the same time, these are works of original scholarship, opening up new areas of Canadian history for students and academics. So, the books contain the documentation necessary to guide students to the key sources, but are not so weighed down with scholarly paraphernalia as to lose their clarity and readability. Canadians, whether or not they are scholars, are growing ever more concerned to discover their real history. We hope this series will contribute to that discovery.

S. F. Wise
Michael S. Cross

Preface

The primary purpose of this study is to examine the economic and social conditions of the working class population of Montreal during a period which is commonly regarded as a time of national expansion and prosperity. The term "working class," as used in this book, refers to the two-thirds of the population of the city whose income was derived from wages as distinct from self-employed or salaried workers. The inquiry is based exclusively on printed sources and looks at working class life from the outside. At one stage of the research I had hoped to modify this coldly analytical approach by using the techniques of oral history. Trial interviews were, however, both disappointing and incredibly time consuming and this approach had to be abandoned. The study is, therefore, a picture of the socio-economic system within which the working class lived, rather than a portrait of working class life.

The secondary purpose of the study is an attempt to determine which aspects of the socio-economic system were peculiar to Montreal and the Province of Quebec. This emerged both from the data and from the traditions of Canadian historiography. Government reports and the comments of other contemporary observers were almost always couched in comparative terms and no one who has spent the last ten years teaching Canadian history could fail to be aware of the debate on the origins of Quebec's "backwardness." The reader should perhaps be warned that I had long ago chosen sides in this debate. Ever since reading Albert Faucher and Maurice Lamontagne's article on the "History of Industrial Development in Quebec" in the late fifties, I have been firmly convinced that historians have paid far too much attention to alleged "cultural" differences between Quebec and the rest of Canada and far too little attention to economic questions. To isolate properly, never mind understand, the unique characteristics of any society, the historian must develop a rigorous comparative framework and this is something we have all failed to do.

Certainly no such systematic comparative analysis is undertaken here. Instead there are occasional references to conditions in other North American urban centres and some attempt to explain these observed differences in economic terms. The result is not satisfactory by any means, but perhaps some different questions about the development of Quebec and Montreal have been raised.

A number of aspects of working-class life are not included. Crime, prostitution, venereal disease, alcoholism, and other by-products of a culture of poverty are ignored because no consistent body of evidence for dealing with them was discovered. Statistics on these subjects are so inadequate that no broad picture could be drawn and I was loathe to rely on the occasional descriptive commentary. Much the same problem exists with regard to the daily routine of housewives, a topic which I was greatly interested in writing about.

No one is more aware than I am of the limitations of this study. It is a broad survey, based exclusively on printed sources. Each of the chapters might well form the basis for a sizable monograph. My hope is that the book will assist in opening new areas to historical investigation.

Acknowledgements

The idea of writing a book on social conditions in Montreal originated in the early sixties when I was writing my M.A. thesis for John Irwin Cooper. Professor Cooper was the ideal research director and those sessions across his desk have always seemed to me to be a model for good teaching and learning. I was writing political history at that time but conversations with Cooper about the history of Montreal suggested that there was a whole new kind of history to be explored. In 1963 I was fortunate enough to be invited to join the excellent history department which Geoff Adams and Don Savage had created at Loyola College. There, in an atmosphere which was both intellectually exciting and harmonious, I learned my trade. To all of the original group, now scattered, I owe a special debt. To Dave O'Brien, who shared a seminar in North American historiography with me, I owe more than I can ever acknowledge. The same may be said for Bob Vogel who got me into history in the first place and has remained a close friend.

While I was at Loyola, I was also teaching a course at McGill, maintaining my connection with John Cooper and the McGill Department. In those years I did some work on the material included in this book and portions of the first chapter are based on a paper I gave to the Montreal Historical Society in 1966. My focus at that time was on urban progressivism and a number of my Loyola students wrote honours essays on aspects of that theme applied to Montreal. I have acknowledged some of their work in the footnotes but I would like to add an additional word of thanks for their role in helping to convince me that progressivism, in Montreal at least, had little to do with progress. Michel Gauvin, who worked as my research assistant in an earlier phase of this study, and Daniel Russel, who wrote an M.A. thesis on Ames, deserve special thanks.

A number of people have read and commented on the manuscript. Cameron Nish, Marcel Hamelin, Ken Dewar, Michael

Piva, Robin Burns and Steve Scheinberg have all helped me to clarify my ideas though they share no responsibility for errors or ambiguities. The editors of the series, Syd Wise and Michael Cross, gave me the benefit of their advice and a much needed deadline. The Centre de Recherche en Histoire Économique du Canada Français provided a grant in the first stages of the research and I gratefully acknowledge that assistance. Christine Knaus typed the final draft and was always willing to meet my deadlines. The secretarial staff at the University of Victoria worked on large parts of the first draft. They were one of the main reasons why our stay at Victoria was productive as well as enjoyable.

The subject of this book has not been a matter of entirely academic interest to me. My maternal grandfather was recruited by the Grand Trunk Railway in 1905. He left England with a wife and four young children and settled in Verdun. As a skilled cabinetmaker and strong trade unionist, he earned enough to maintain his family at a level well above the average. My father came to Montreal in 1924 and found his first job in a textile mill where at age seventeen he earned the princely sum of twelve cents an hour. He later found work in the engineering department of Mother Bell and I grew up in Notre Dame de Grâce, that refuge for those who "made it" by becoming white collar workers. In the course of this study I have come to realize that the university degrees and high salaries of my brothers and I were obtained by years of hard work and sacrifice on the part of our parents.

My wife Linda sacrificed her own work to give me time to write. For that I can try and pay her back but the other things I owe to her are beyond calculation.

T.L.

The Anatomy of Poverty

Chapter 1

The City Below the Hill

During the autumn and early winter of 1896, a young Montreal businessman, Herbert Brown Ames, employed a number of "enumerators" to undertake "A Sociological Study of a Portion of the City of Montreal, Canada." Ames assembled the results of the questionnaires into a short book called *The City Below the Hill*, which was published in 1897.[1] The district surveyed contained thirty-eight thousand people and the residents, mainly working class, were "evenly divided as to nationality, one-third French Canadian, one-third English, and one-third Irish." It was, Ames said, an opportunity "to study a class rather than a race."

In the introduction to the book the author wrote,

> . . . those who study city life are each day more fully persuaded that ordinary urban conditions are demoralizing and that no portion of the community can be allowed to deteriorate without danger to the whole, when it is being proven over and over again by enlightened municipalities that the public health can be conserved, morals improved and lives saved by a right knowledge of local conditions and the proper measures for their amelioration, it is opportune that the citizens of Montreal should, for a time, cease discussing the slums of London, the beggars of Paris and the tenement house evils of New York and endeavour to learn something about themselves and to understand more perfectly the conditions present in their very midst.

The conditions present in the very midst of the same city inhabited by "the captains of industry, the owners of real estate and those who labour with brain rather than hand" were described in minute detail with the aid of numerous maps. The section chosen by Ames for his survey was one of the older industrial quarters of Montreal. Its northwestern boundary was the C.P.R. tracks leading into

The City Below and the City Above, 1896.

Windsor Station. A block to the southeast lay the right of way of the Grand Trunk and the extensive yards of Bonaventure Station and two blocks below that the Lachine Canal, the oldest centre of industry in the city, cut through the district. Beyond the canal, Centre Street marked the beginning of Point St. Charles. To the southwest, the still autonomous working class suburbs of Ste. Cunegonde and St. Henri marked the western limit of urbanization, but to the east the old wards of the city stretched along the river for several miles.

Rue Notre Dame bisected the City Below the Hill and was the axis of all the *quartiers* of the old city. It was paved for most of its length by 1897 with a mixture of cobblestones and wooden blocks.[2] Like most of the other main streets, it was festooned with the overhead wires of the Montreal Street Railway Company. At night the glare of arc lamps and the glow of the remaining gas lights cast dark shadows over most of the street. Notre Dame was lined with one and two-storey structures, mainly brick, intermingled with the more substantial greystone and shanty-built wooden houses. Sewer lines served most of the area on either side of Notre Dame Street but, despite the municipal by-law that had forbidden the further construction of houses served by the "pit privy" since 1887, over five thousand privy pits remained in existence within city limits and more than half the households in the section surveyed by Ames were "dependant entirely on such accommodation." Since water service reached almost every house in the city, Ames allowed himself a rare expression of emotion in discussing "that insanitary abomination . . . that danger to public health and morals . . . the out-of-door-pit-in-the-ground privy." There is, he wrote,

a map in my office whereon are coloured in yellow all blocks of buildings containing only proper sanitary accommodation, and whereon the presence of the privy abomination is designated by shades of purple, from violet to nearly black according to its prevalence.

This problem was general throughout the working class wards and for eight years Ames was to maintain a campaign (which earned him the title "Water Closet Ames") for the suppression of the pit privy.

The carter's waggon and the horse and carriage were the only means of transportation other than the street railway. The Haymarket was then not the name of a square but an important commercial facility. There were three thousand horse stables within city limits in 1899 as well as five hundred cow stables. The Municipal Board of Health recommended that cow stables, at least, be banned within city limits.[3]

17

The condition of the streets of the city occasioned much comment. Since only 27 of the 178 miles of streets were paved "dust in the autumn is very bad and the mud wears out the streets quicker than the traffic does." According to the City Surveyor the dust also impaired the health of the city.[4] Medical officers were more explicit. Elzéar Pelletier, Secretary of the Provincial Board of Health, complained that the streets "were in an intolerable state though tolerated" and that the lanes were used as "refuse dumps."[5]

The city-owned water supply, while generally available, was of a poor quality. It was unfiltered and untreated and while it was "pure during ordinary times, it becomes dangerous during spring and fall." The main reservoir "leaked badly" and the boom which blocked floating refuse at the entrance was "in a state of decay."[6] Householders who did not pay their water tax had the supply of this dubious commodity cut off.

Little attention had been paid to city planning in Montreal and one of the most serious deficiencies of the working class wards was the lack of parks and open spaces. The thirty-eight thousand inhabitants of the western section of the lower city shared two public squares, Richmond and St. Patrick's. The twenty-six thousand residents of St. Louis possessed tiny Viger Square, in St. Laurent Ward there were the two acres of Dufferin Square and the pattern was similar elsewhere.[7] Montreal did, of course, have its "Great Park," Mount Royal. Frederic Law Olmstead, who designed Mount Royal Park, considered it to be one of the best in North America:

> Rising in the rear of the city ... its landscape is most captivating ... 462 acres laid out with drives, rustic steps and seats ... footpaths leading in every direction to wander amidst an undergrowth of ferns and flowers ... the summit can be reached winding around the mountain side ... on the eastern side of the mountain there is an incline railroad by which special cars carry passengers to the lookout for a small fee... [8]

But Mount Royal was remote from the everyday life of the city. Like St. Helen's Island, which was reached by ferry, it was a place for family outings on very special days. A newer park located just to the north of some of the more congested areas of the city had more potential as a "people's park." Logan's Farm or Lafontaine Park was being transformed in the late 1890s. The beautiful lagoons, the feature attraction, were being installed and the landscaping was largely complete. Yet the life of the majority of the population could only have been marginally affected. The playground movement, which was spreading across North America from the "sand garden" and "outdoor gymnasium" created in Boston during the 1880s, had not yet reached Montreal.

The streets of the city, however, hummed with activity. The local bar was the chief recreational facility available to adults and there was one in almost every block. Ames counted 105 licensed saloons and 87 liquor selling groceries in the survey area and claimed that even if the ones located adjacent to railway stations were eliminated there was a "licensed liquor outlet, no one knows how many unlicensed" for every forty-five families.

Herbert Ames approached the problem of the circumstances of working class life with what he felt was scientific objectivity. His purpose in writing the book was spelled out in the introduction:

There are among the dwellers of "the city above the hill" not a few, we believe, who have the welfare of their fellow-men at heart, who realize there is no influence more elevating than the proper home, who acknowledge that there is a need for improvement in the matter of housing the working classes of the city and who would be willing to assist any movement of a semi-philanthropic character having for its object the erection of proper homes for the families of working men. These persons are business men. They are not those who take things for granted. They require to have demonstrated to them in black and white the need for local action and the conditions – changing with every locality – to which it would be needful to conform to meet the needs of the case, and, at the same time, yield reasonable financial returns... 'Philanthropy and five per cent' in Montreal, as elsewhere, can be combined.

Ames had spent four years at Amherst College where he had been a contemporary of men like Robert A. Woods, the founder of Andover Settlement House in Boston, and a prominent writer and social reformer, Robert E. Ely, one of the founders of Prospect Union and the Harvard workingman's college, and a dozen other men who were active in social gospel inspired reform.[9] Ames, like the others, had been influenced by the lectures of President Seelye of Amherst, who attacked the doctrinal individualism of Calvinism and preached an organic conception of society. He had listened to prominent social gospellers like Lyman Abbott and Henry Ward Beecher[10] and was deeply affected by the intense searching for moral purpose that marked

Jacques Cartier Square, 1896.

the college. He had been taught to believe that the wealthy had special responsibilities towards their less fortunate brethren and when, at his father's death, he succeeded to the control of the family shoe factory, he was able to resign from business activity and devote his full energies to municipal affairs. For Ames, reform was to be accomplished by demonstrating the existence of "evils" to men of good will and then working out a businesslike solution which would find support among the established classes. He accepted the wide discrepancies in income, education, and opportunity that existed in the society but believed that at least some abuses of urban-industrial society could be removed by right knowledge and right action.

As a consequence, Ames never raised fundamental questions about wage levels or working conditions. His investigation was designed to prove that the area was "eminently suitable for philanthropic investment," not to show the need for a general reform movement. In developing his case for a model tenement, Ames touched on problems of a more general kind and his statistics provide a convenient point of departure for a study of working class conditions just before the relatively static patterns of late nineteenth century life were disrupted by rapid economic growth and massive immigration to the city.

The industries located in the area surveyed represented a good cross section of Montreal's economic life. Wholesale clothing, boots and shoes, textiles, foodstuffs, cigars, iron and steel, lumber, transportation equipment as well as a host of lesser shops and service facilities provided work for 12,511 men, 3,266 women, and 460 children.[11] Approximately one-third of the labour force lived outside of the area surveyed, so Ames' sample was composed of 7,671 families who were residents. The average family income was eleven dollars per week. The range of weekly income varied from over twenty dollars ($15\frac{1}{3}$ per cent) to under five dollars (11 per cent). These groups, "the well-to-do" and "the submerged tenth," did not "properly belong to the class under study." It was the remainder, the "real industrial class," which required examination.

The average family income of the "real industrial class," $10.00 to $10.25 a week, was based on some combination of earnings from more than one wage earner and the estimate that average weekly wages of $8.25 for a man, $4.50 for a woman and $3.00 for a boy were "not too wide off the mark." A man able to work throughout the year could earn more than $428.00 a year according to these figures. Yet in 1901, a more prosperous year with much fuller employment, manufacturing establishments in Montreal reported average wages for men of $405.00.[12]

21

The figure of $10.25 a week used by Ames was the average income when the breadwinners were working. He himself noted that in addition to the "submerged tenth" the "City Below the Hill" contained "a much larger group who were on the verge of distress" because of "insufficient employment." "Few are the families" he wrote,

> where nothing is earned, although there are such subsisting more or less worthily upon charity. Almost without exception each family has its wage earner, often more than one, and upon the regularity with which the wage earner secures employment depends the scale of living of the family.

Ames' statistics showed that 23 per cent of the "real industrial class" had incomes "which could not be depended on as constant and regular throughout the year . . . the ratio of *nearly one family in four without steady work* [italics in the original] seems alarmingly high and explains much of the poverty."

Income figures have little significance unless measured against some estimate of purchasing power and minimum standard of living. Ames had no clear ideas on how to go about constructing a minimum family budget and he tried to define "the point below which comfort ends and poverty commences" in a rather curious way. "It is difficult," he wrote,

> to determine what shall constitute the low water mark of decent subsistence . . . Since a dollar a day is regarded as the minimum wage for an unskilled labourer it would seem that six dollars a week might be taken as the point below which comfort ends . . . But . . . since few are those among this class of labourers who can count upon regular work . . . we may safely fix the limit of decent subsistence at $5.00 per week.

For Ames the wage system could not possibly produce poverty; therefore, persons who worked more or less regularly for the minimum wage could not be poor. By the standards used for measuring poverty, developed in the following chapter, the vast majority of the population of the "City Below the Hill" are classified as poor.

The dimension of life in "The City Below the Hill" that Ames explored in the greatest detail was housing. He was determined to build a "model tenement" in Montreal and had commissioned the survey primarily to bolster his case for "semiphilanthropic investment." By 1897 the "model tenement" idea had been tested in a number of American cities, most successfully in Brooklyn where Alfred T. White had conducted his experiments in "philanthropy plus five per cent." In the same year that Ames began his preparations to build "Diamond Court," a project for the accommodation of forty families, on William Street, the New York Association for Improving the Conditions of the Poor (A.I.C.P.) organized the "City and Suburban Homes Association" with a capitalization of $1,000,000 as a limited dividend corporation to build model tenements. Ames had observed the American experience closely and was determined to avoid the mistakes that had been made. In particular, he warned against building "dwellings too high priced for the neighborhood." Though this would "benefit the locality," the mass of the people "would live as before."

Ames began by defining the housing standards he was seeking:

I think we will all agree that the ideal home is one where the front door is used by but one family, where the house faces upon a through street, where water closet accommodation is provided and where there are as many rooms allotted to a family as there are persons composing it. That this ideal is by no means obtained goes without saying.

The average house in the district was a duplex, for the lofty tenements of New York and Chicago did not exist in Montreal. Ames regarded the independence and self-reliance, which he felt these small houses promoted, outweighed the disadvantages of "high rentals or mean accommodations" which low density housing caused. Ten per cent of the total housing stock consisted of rear tenements. "The typical rear tenement," Ames wrote,

is either an ancient wooden cottage of the rural *habitant* type or a two-storey building encased in refuse bricks and reached by rickety wooden stairs or galleries. It is high time in Montreal, that the majority of these hovels were condemned as unfit for habitation . . . It is already within the power of City Council to prevent the erection of further buildings of this type . . . we must go a step further and give to civic authority, as representing the public welfare, the right to interfere with what are known as private interests and vested rights, when these latter are, as in this case, a menace to the welfare of the community. The rear tenement must go.

The average family in the area lived in a flat containing 5.02 rooms. This figure compared favourably with almost all industrial cities of comparable size. When broken down into segments, the

Typical blocks of flats, St. Denis and St. Zotiques Streets, 1922.

statistics showed that 30 per cent shared six rooms, 40 per cent five rooms, and 30 per cent four rooms. The average rental for these flats worked out to $8.75 per month or 18 per cent of monthly income. The "poor and the well-to-do" paid from 20-25 per cent of their income for housing, the "real industrial class" closer to 16 per cent. It is fair to conclude that with the exception of a few areas such as Griffintown, where 45 per cent of the population had three rooms or less to share among a family of five, the housing was not overcrowded by contemporary standards. Equally it may be concluded that rent as a percentage of income was not out of line.

It is also evident that Montreal's low density housing kept the density per acre figure well below European and many North American urban levels. The section surveyed had a density of 94 persons to the acre. This calculation was based on excluding non-residential areas. The city's figures for density per acre did not match this calculation; its estimate for the wards, which were included in the section surveyed by Ames, were 35 and 47 persons per acre (Ste. Anne and St. Antoine Wards).

The wards to the east were much more densely populated. According to the City Surveyor, the average in St. Louis was 117 to the acre, St. James 96, St. Lawrence 67, St. Mary's 63, and St. Jean Baptiste 56.[13] Within the area surveyed by Ames, density went as high as 300 per acre and averaged 200 per acre throughout much of the district. Two hundred persons per acre in a city of small homes meant that very little open space had been left on the building lots. Ames concluded the chapter by noting that there was 5 to 7 per cent vacancy rate in the district.

A further chapter was devoted to the death rate, "the test to which cities of the civilized world, by common consent, annually submit themselves." Montreal's death rate had been steadily declining but it was still among the highest in the civilized world in the 1890s. The figure of 24.81 deaths per thousand (1895) which Ames used, compared to a rate of 20 per thousand in London and Paris, 19.4 in Rome, 18.1 in Brussels, 24.02 in Boston, and 23.52 in New York. By 1898 New York had lowered its rate to 19.0 while Montreal's rate had declined to 22.9. Toronto by comparison had a death rate of only 15.2.[14]

There was a wide variance in death rates between different parts of the city. St. Jean Baptiste Ward had 35.51 deaths per thousand, St. Mary's 33.20, and St. Gabriel 32.32 compared to 22.47 for the "City Below the Hill" and less than 13 per thousand in the upper section of St. Antoine Ward, "The City Above the Hill." Ames was able to establish a strong correlation between the death rate and housing and sanitary conditions.

One of the most obvious omissions in Ames' study was the question of infant mortality. Montreal was the most dangerous city in the civilized world to be born in. Between 1899 and 1901, 26.76 per cent of all new born children died before they were one year old. This was more than double the figure for New York City, and it was customarily cited as being lower than only one large city –Calcutta.[15] The death of children under one year made up 43 per cent of the total deaths in the city in 1897. These statistics were largely the result of unsafe water, impure milk, and the limited use of vaccination against smallpox and diphtheria. The secretary of the Provincial Board of Health commented that,

> ... the thought of having little angels in heaven can only afford consolation when one is satisfied that everything possible was done ... there should be no misconception on the subject, the use of anti-diphtheria serum has not yet become general in our province.[16]

In Montreal even smallpox vaccination had not "become general." City Health officials estimated that the 2,094 primary vaccinations they had performed on babies in 1899 represented only one-fifth of the number of births in the city. One of the schools in Ames' district was reported as having 39 per cent of its pupils without vaccinations.[17]

Ames also ignored the question of the conditions in which the wage earners earned their living. The six-day week was of course the general rule, though some employers allowed a half day off on Saturday, providing an extra hour was added on to the other five days. During the middle 1890s "short time" layoffs and plant shutdowns were normal in the winter months. The working day averaged between ten and twelve hours, though women and children in factories were not permitted to work more than ten hours a day, six days a week, unless a special permit had been obtained for a period "not exceeding six weeks."[18] This rule did not apply to women and children employed in retail shops or other establishments not covered by the Industrial Establishments Act of 1893.

In 1897 there were three factory inspectors charged with the task of enforcing the I.E.A. and the "By-laws of the Quebec Board of Health Relating to the Sanitary Conditions of Industrial Establishments (1895)," for Montreal and all of western Quebec. They were required to examine all "manufactories, works, workshops, work yards, mills of every kind and their dependencies." The main work of the inspectors was to report on the causes of industrial accidents and enforce the child labour laws which stated that "the age of admission to work in factories not classified as dangerous or unhealthy is twelve for boys and fourteen for girls." Proof of age, in the form of a statement signed by a parent or guardian, was required in case of doubt. The factory inspectors could require that one hour be alloted for lunch. They could attempt to enforce the rule that 400 cubic feet of air per workman was available, that there were separate sanitary accommodations for men and women, that a temperature of 60 to 72 degrees Fahrenheit was maintained and that there was adequate ventilation, drainage, freedom from dirt and dust, and appropriate fire escape mechanisms. In theory, offending employers could be fined $200 for each contravention of the Act and $6 per day until the faults were remedied. In practice, since the inspector was required to institute court proceedings himself, a mixture of persuasion and threats was used to try to reform the more obvious abuses.

The Chief Factory Inspector, Louis Guyon, was a dedicated and conscientious individual whose role as a lobbyist in factory reform will be examined in detail. His report for 1897 includes the following observations:

There have been very few infractions to note in regard to the employment of children under age; the limit of 12 years for boys being so low that there is hardly any desire among manufacturers to employ them younger.... From the standpoint of the prevention of accidents ... inspection is very important. It is impossible not to feel a profound sense of pity for these poor victims of labour. For the inspector, it is the part of his duty which calls for the most effort and perseverance to find in the first place the means of protection best suited to the circumstances and next to convince employers that such improvements form part of well understood progress and that in protecting their employees against accidents they are protecting themselves from an economical point of view.[19]

The improvement of working conditions and the achievement of a living wage are changes which are normally associated with successful trade union activity. For a time in the 1880s it had appeared as if the Knights of Labour might successfully organize the city's workers along industrial lines. The assemblies of the Knights broke down the barrier between linguistic groups and united skilled and unskilled labour. Their high point was reached in 1887 when there were thirty-eight assemblies or locals in the city. The failure of the Knights to achieve significant gains in a series of strikes coupled with the hard times of the later eighties led to a rapid decline in membership and there were only four Knights of Labour locals left in 1891.

By 1897 only the craft unions with international affiliation survived as viable associations. Such union locals possessed little bargaining power and less staying power. The Department of Labour's first survey of trade unions in 1901 listed sixty locals in Montreal, one-third of which had been organized since 1897.[20] Organized labour participated in the annual Labour Day Parade and sent delegates to the Trades and Labour Council convention, but it was simply not a force to be reckoned with in the quiet times of the 1890s.

In the absence of an effective trade union movement, an alternative path to improved working class life was the universal curative of North America, education. Eighteen hundred and ninety-seven is frequently regarded as a crucial year in the history of education in the Province of Quebec. The newly formed Liberal administration of Felix-Gabriel Marchand was committed to fulfilling the *rouge* dream of a Ministry of Public Instruction. The passage of this bill in the assembly and its subsequent rejection by the *bleu* dominated Legislative Council postponed the creation of a ministry of education for sixty-five years. For the resident of the working class sections of Montreal the great debates over public versus religious control of education must have seemed of little interest. Education was neither compulsory nor free and though the school inspectors and the Superintendent of Public Instruction insisted that the city's schools were generally excellent,[21] there is little evidence to support their view and much to contradict it. The Provincial Health Board was concerned with "the deplorable sanitary conditions of the schools," and noted that while ideal standards called for two hundred and fifty cubic feet of space per pupil and Quebec's laws demanded one hundred and fifty cubic feet, the average in Montreal was only seventy-five cubic feet. The Board reported that little attention was paid to siting, orientation to the sun, ventilation or heating and that many schools lacked fire escapes.[22] Ninety per cent of the teachers had less than eleven years of schooling[23] and their salaries were among the lowest in North America. Over 80 per cent of the total enrolment in primary schools was registered in Grades one to three and less than 3 per cent of the students were in Grade six.[24] Provincial government expenditure on education was at the lowest point in the province's history, having declined in absolute terms from $155,000 in 1883 to $153,000 in 1901 and from seventy-five cents per student to fifty-six cents over the same period.[25] The frequent comments of the factory inspectors on the illiteracy of children in the work force add to the picture of an educational system which had little relevance for working class children.

Even the goals of the Superintendent of Public Instruction, to teach "great respect for paternal, civil and religious authority . . . warn against intemperance and extravagance that impoverish our country . . . avoid quarrels and law suits . . . show the benefits conferred by agriculture,"[26] could not have been very adequately fulfilled in such a system.

* * *

The typical Montreal family of 1897 was made up of a husband, wife and three children who lived in a five-room, cold water flat located on a narrow, densely populated side street in what is now the inner core of the city. The husband, who hoped to be able to work sixty hours a week, fifty-two weeks a year, was more likely to find himself faced with "short time" if not a layoff, especially during the winter months. Even if regular work was available, the average wage earner could not provide his family with more than a bare subsistence.

The insecurity of family finances brought enormous pressure to bear upon the children who were expected to enter the work force at the earliest possible age. Large numbers of children were involved in part-time work as messengers, delivery boys, newsboys, and in home workshops.[27] Official statistics vastly underestimated the extent of paid child labour and did not attempt to account for the unpaid labour of hundreds of young girls who were used as full-time baby sitters. The large numbers of ten to fourteen-year-old girls who were not in school and are not accounted for in the labour force were often taking care of the home while their mothers worked.[28] Ames' figures indicate that one in every five adult workers was a woman. The working class woman was required to seek employment in the textile mills, tobacco companies, food processing concerns, retail stores, and in domestic service. Her wages, low as they were, often made the difference between bare subsistence and a modest "prosperity" for her family.

Chapter 2

The Real Incomes of the Working Class

The life of the working class family in the 1890s was marked by poverty and insecurity but there were aspects of the 1890s which, in retrospect, might have made the decade seem like the proverbial "good old days." The population of Montreal had grown steadily but slowly since 1880. Prices had remained remarkably stable or had even declined during the previous twenty years. Wages had held firm or moved slightly upwards. After 1897 conditions began to change. The wheat boom of the early twentieth century brought prosperity, of a kind, to Montreal. The population almost doubled in the years before World War I and by 1929 a small city with a population of less than 250,000 had become a metropolis containing a million people. The boom was accompanied by new threats to the precarious existence of the working class family: inflation and a massive pool of immigrant labour competing for jobs, housing, municipal services, and space in the city's schools. The working class population of Montreal found that growth in the size and aggregate wealth of the city did not result in a significant improvement in their standard of living.

`The most important single measure of the standard of living for an urban population is the amount of real income available to family units. This chapter is therefore concerned with an analysis of the incomes of hourly wage earners over the thirty year period. The question of real income as distinct from income in current dollars is approached by establishing a minimum budget for a family of five and relating changes in the pricing of that standardized budget to changes in the incomes received by wage earners.

Data on incomes is extremely sketchy before 1921 and the estimates offered here are only rough approximations. The censuses of 1921 and 1931 provide much fuller information but they were both taken in years of high unemployment and the figures are not really representative of incomes during the war years or most of the 1920s. An attempt has been made to allow for this but again estimates can only be approximate.

The general conclusion drawn from the data is that the vast majority of families in Montreal in the years under review was unable to reach the minimum income level unless there was relatively full employment and at least two wage earners per family unit. For the two-thirds of the adult male labour force employed as hourly wage earners there was little chance of earning sufficient income, even at maturity, to provide an average family with the minimum standard of living. Certainly if the modern Statistics Canada definition of poverty – "any family or individual spending more than seventy per cent of total income on food, clothing and shelter" – is used, then poverty was the common experience of the majority of the population of Montreal.

The evidence upon which these assertions are based is admittedly incomplete but the statistical data which are available, together with much descriptive evidence, strongly points to this conclusion. Before examining the information on incomes, it is necessary to evaluate the minimum standard used as a measure of poverty. Three different budgets for a typical family of five were considered. The Federal Department of Labour began to publish a weekly budget for a family of five in 1910.[1] The primary purpose of the budget, which is reproduced in Appendix A, was to provide a basis for tracing changes in the cost of food, fuel, and rent in Canadian cities. It was thought that items analysed represented between 60 and 80 per cent of ordinary expenditure (the figure of 70 per cent has been used in making calculations for this study). The budget was based on data gathered by the U.S. Department of Labour in 1901-02[2] and no survey of actual expenditure patterns in Canada was made. It was not until 1926 that two separate surveys of the cost of living in Montreal were undertaken.

The Family Welfare Association survey of 1926 was prepared by a committee which first established minimum requirements and then priced items in corner stores. The budget excluded health care, luxuries such as tobacco or amusements of any kind, household utensils, union dues, savings, insurance, and all other non-essentials and reached the conclusion that $1,101.76 was the absolute minimum required for a family with three children under fourteen. This budget, which is also reproduced in Appendix A, may be best described as a bare subsistence budget, somewhat above the sum of $856.00 that the Family Welfare Association was able to allot to a dependent family of five, but well below the minimum which the Canadian Brotherhood of Railway Employees suggested in 1926. In preparing their investigation of the cost of living in ten Canadian cities, the C.B.R.E. used somewhat different methods.[3] They adopted the "Minimum Quantity Budget for Health and Decency" used by the U.S. Bureau of Labor Statistics and repriced all items for each Canadian city. The result was an estimate of $2,163.42 as the sum necessary for a family of five in Montreal (see Appendix A).

The Department of Labour family budget figure for 1926 is almost exactly between these two guidelines, calling for an expenditure of $1,590 to meet ordinary needs when the basic items are calculated as 70 per cent of the total requirement. It would not seem unreasonable to use the Department of Labour family budget as a guide to the approximate amount of income required to lead a life somewhere between the barest subsistence and health and decency. This allows us to trace changes in the poverty line back to 1900 without undertaking the task of trying to price the items in the other budgets over a thirty-year period.

The published census reports which provide the basic information on incomes used in this study do not include comprehensive information on incomes until 1921. The data in the 1901 Census is particularly limiting; since all workers of whatever age and both sexes are included within the statement of wages paid, only the manufacturing sector of the Montreal economy can be analysed. When manufacturing industries, which contained insignificant numbers of women and children, are isolated, it is possible to compute the average annual income of 6,543 male workers in a list of industries which excludes virtually all of the classically low wage sectors of the economy. The average income for this group came to $405 per year, or $7.78 per week.[4] The Department of Labour budget, worked back to 1900, called for a weekly expenditure of $9.64 for basic items or $13.77 for the total needs of an "ordinary family of five."[5] It is evident that even if the average male worker had a working wife or child, total family income could not quite reach this level. The average wages of women in Montreal were very close to the national average of $190 per year, or $3.65 a week.[6] Young boys and girls earned even less.

The same method applied to the Census of 1911 allows the isolation of 8,643 adult male workers who averaged $549 a year, or $10.55 a week.[7] Price increases over the ten years had raised the necessary expenditure level to $12.82 a week for basics and $18.31 for the total budget. Average incomes of women and children in the labour force had reached $6.00 and $4.00 per week respectively. The income figures for 1911, unlike the ones used in 1901, can be checked against the annual earnings of "Heads of Families in Specified Occupations" in Montreal. This Census table indicates that the average income for five categories of skilled building tradesmen was $13.70 a week. Building construction labourers averaged $10.21 a week. Trainmen, traditionally among the highest paid wage earners, received an average of $18.67 and were the only group surveyed who earned enough to place their families above the poverty line used in this study.[8]

Nineteen hundred and eleven was a year of great activity in the economy of Montreal and high levels of employment continued into 1912. In that year, the Committee which organized the Child Welfare Exhibition developed a family budget which can serve as a method of checking our poverty line. The Committee suggested that an unskilled labourer could earn $1.75 a day or $550 a year at the going rates. It noted, however, that

> To get this much . . . a man must have continuous work (six days a week, fifty-two weeks a year) with no sickness, no changes in jobs, and he must not waste his money on drink or dissipation. Granted all this he can give a family of five a mere existence. . . . No allowance is here made for sickness, recreation, church, house furnishings, lectures and savings.[9]

The Committee attempted to prepare a family budget based on $555 a year, but it noted that its allowance for rent meant that "a man must live in unsanitary quarters, sometimes below street level" and that the allotment for food was not sufficient for a family of five, even if the exacting methods of the Committee's Domestic Science experts were applied. "How," the report asked, "shall an untrained girl who went to work at 14 or earlier, know enough to prepare the meals for her family with such rigid foresight?"[10]

The Committee also sponsored an investigation of "several hundred working girls employed in factories." The report suggested that since the girls were "more highly paid than the average they could understand an elaborate questionnaire." The results of this investigation showed that,

> The girl who goes to work to earn a little pin money is largely a fiction. It is true that a large number of girls live at home but that does not save them much expense; in most cases they must help with the family support. By far the largest number of these girls receive wages from $4 to $6 per week not counting subtractions made for fines or for days of sickness.[11]

The work done by the Child Welfare Exhibition Committee seems to confirm the validity of our income and expenditure calculations. Average family income was most probably well above the $550 per year level, but below the $952 required to rise above the poverty line. The "ordinary expenditure" level could only be approached if there was more than one wage earner per family.

The years between 1901 and 1912 had not been a period of continuous prosperity and full employment. The heavy incidence of seasonal unemployment in Montreal was a characteristic of every year and is accounted for by measuring annual rather than weekly income, but business recessions such as occurred in 1907-08 must have had catastrophic effects on low income families. Not only was unemployment far greater but short-time, half-time, and wage cutbacks were standard devices used to cut down on costs. For example, the Dominion Textile Company, which paid its mill workers an average of ninety-two cents a day in 1907, decided to reduce the hours of work in the fall of that year as demand slackened. The employees, who endured a winter of short time, were then confronted with a 10 per cent wage cut in the spring of 1908. A strike followed but the only result was the promise of a restoration of previous wage rates "when trade improves."[12]

The depression which began in 1913 and continued until late 1915 was far more severe than the financial crisis of 1907-08. One of the provincial factory inspectors reported that he had never seen so much unemployment[13] and the reports of labour unions on the unemployment of their members bear out this observation.[14]

The war eventually brought a return to a high level of production in the existing factories of Montreal as well as the creation of new war-related industries. A labour shortage developed in 1916 and more women and children were drawn into the full time labour force. Wages began to move steadily upwards for most classes of workers. The Department of Labour's index numbers for weekly wages illustrate this trend clearly. Averages for the 21 classes of labour sampled increased by 10 points in 1916, 21 points in 1917 and 15 points in 1918. These averages are representative of changes in Montreal where "Common Labour in Factories" obtained an average increase of 20 per cent between 1915 and 1918. Machinists and iron moulders obtained hourly increases of more than 20 per cent in the last two years of the war as did skilled workers in the building trades.[15]

These unprecedented gains were obtained in the context of

an incredible inflationary spiral which further depressed the standard of living. Between 1915 and 1918 the cost of living rose by more than 40 per cent. At the end of 1916, Felix Marois, an official in the Quebec Department of Labour, described the plight of the wage earner in these terms:

> ... the cost of living continues to rise with a fearful rapidity ... the average cost of mere necessities for a workman's family of five or six is $60 per month ... the majority of workmen do not earn more than $15 per week. Consequently it is not so surprising to see children obliged to leave school and go to work at the age of fourteen or fifteen years. Their wages are very low but in many instances they are imperatively needed for the family's support.[16]

The majority of workmen who did not earn more than $15 per week needed $16.25 per week in 1916 to pay for the *three basic items* in the Department of Labour's "Family Budget." The rampant wartime inflation persisted throughout 1919 and into 1920. The cost of living peaked in 1920 at $22.38 for the three basic items or $31.97 for the full budget, then declined to just over the $21 ($30 per week for the full budget) mark where it remained throughout the rest of the decade.

The break in the inflationary trend was due to the general collapse of "prosperity" in mid-1920. Mass unemployment of a degree similar to the 1913-15 period struck the city's labour force. Unemployment statistics reported by Quebec trade unions reflect the severity of the crash. In May of 1920 only 2.54 per cent of their membership was unemployed; by November the rate had reached 13.83 per cent and by May of 1921 26.54 per cent of trade union members were listed as unemployed.[17]

The Census of 1921 which surveys the year ending June 1, 1921, captures a picture of the Canadian labour force during a year of profound disruption in the pattern of employment and income. Annual earnings for many in the labour force may have been significantly lower than they were in the previous year. The schedules used in the 1921 census allow us to make a very general reconstruction of occupational and income categories and it is unfortunate that the decennial census was taken in a year which was not typical of either the wartime period or the relative stability of most of the 1920s.

The method of grouping used here is adopted from Leonard C. Marsh's *Employment Research*[18] in which four major categories of employment are utilized. Marsh, working from the 1931 Census, removed all owners, managers, foremen, officials and professional occupations from Census data and grouped them together in one category. Labourers and clerical workers constituted a second and third category and all other workers were placed in a fourth classification. The Tables in the 1921 Census are not fully comparable with those published in 1931 and no attempt to trace changes in the composition of the labour force is undertaken here. The following table illustrates the percentage breakdown of occupational groups of male workers in Montreal in 1921.[19]

		1921 Male Workers
I	Managers & Superintendents, Professional Workers, Foremen etc.	19%
II	Labourers	12%
III	Clerical Workers	11%
IV	All Others (Hourly wage earners)	56%

Labourers and other hourly wage workers made up more than two thirds of all the gainfully occupied in 1921. If we examine the average annual incomes of hourly wage earners taking only those workers between the ages of twenty-five and forty-nine, the peak earning years, the result is an average annual income of less than $1,100 per year or $21.15 a week. Labourers earned considerably less, $900 per year, $17.30 a week. These figures fit closely with the reported earnings of "Heads of Families in Specified Occupations" in Montreal reported in the 1921 Census. Five categories of building trades employees recorded incomes averaging $1,132.00, "Labourers" reported $959.00, and "Domestic and personal workers" $1,035.00.[20] Male clerical workers between the ages of 25 and 49 averaged incomes of $1,200 per year or $23.00 per week. It is doubtful that much in the way of a middle class style of life was possible despite the colour of the collar worn by clerical workers. Foremen earned an average of $1,563 per year while the average for managers and superintendents was $2,640.[21] Even if we assume that average annual earnings for the 1920-21 were 20 per cent lower than in 1919-20 due to unemployment, the average adjusted incomes for hourly wage earners would have been $1,220 a year or $23.40 a week, still well below the minimum.

On the basis of the data it is necessary to conclude that the average annual incomes for adult male workers in occupations

Construction gang, Ontario Street, 1912.

which involved two thirds of the city's labour force were from 20 to 30 per cent below the poverty line.

The 1921 Census data on the families of wage earners classified according to the occupation of the male head indicates that the average family was composed of 4.5 persons and 1.4 wage earners. Family income for hourly wage employees in "Manufacturing" averaged $1,484 or $28.54 per week, in "Construction" the average was $1,482 or $28.50 a week, in "Transportation" the average was $1,535 or $29.52 a week.[22] Average family income was much closer to the minimum budget in 1921 than it ever had been before. Given price stability, higher levels of employment and continued participation in the labour force by children of high school age the average working class family might be able to make ends meet. However the depression which began in 1920 continued throughout 1921 and into 1922. By December of 1921 Quebec trade unions were still reporting that more than one quarter of their members were unemployed.[23] The 5 per cent decline in the cost of living that accompanied the depression undoubtedly helped those who kept their jobs so long as they were not confronted with wage cuts. Wage cuts were common, however, at least according to the Quebec section of the Trades and Labour Council, which reported that

almost all unions have had to combat wage reductions. Only the well organized trades have been able to withstand the battle, the others having had to accept reductions and as consequence have lost membership.[24]

By mid-1922 unemployment was reported to be down to normal seasonal levels.[25] The Industrial Relations Committee of the Canadian Manufacturer's Association raised an interesting question about the nature of current "prosperity" and the decline of unemployment. In its Report for the year 1923 the Committee suggested that "unemployment has declined not because of increased activity but because of a very large exodus to the United States"[26] which was estimated at one hundred and eighty thousand persons. No quantitative information on emigration from Montreal is available but there are some indications that full recovery to wartime or pre-1913 levels of activity was postponed until 1925 and it may be safely assumed that the city contributed its share to the three hundred thousand Canadians who left the country between 1920 and 1925.[27]

Wage levels seem to have remained remarkably constant during the period 1922 to 1930, the index number for Manufacturing varying by less than two points over the eight years.[28] Wage stability was accompanied by a reduction in the total hours worked though reductions in the length of the work week in Montreal were very slight. The Department of Labour's survey of the hours of labour in Canada for 1929 suggest that a work week of fifty-two hours was normal for wage earners in the city in that year.[29]

The Census of 1931 records data for the year beginning June 1, 1930. Annual income statistics for that twelve month period were strongly influenced by high rates of unemployment and are bound to be significantly lower than in previous years. Forty-four per cent of all male wage earners in Montreal "lost time" during that year and the average time lost for those affected was twenty-three weeks.[30] In view of this it is difficult to use the material in the 1931 Census for analysing incomes in the late 1920s but an estimate of the differential between reported incomes in 1930-31 and potential incomes at "full employment" in the late 1920s must be attempted. The following discussion of working class incomes is based directly on the work of Leonard Marsh in the McGill Social Research Series.

Marsh's study of income statistics for Montreal wage earners in 1930-31 begins with a calculation of the average money earnings of all employees in the city.

Sex and Age Differentials in Earnings: Montreal 1930-31
(All Wage and Salary Earners)[31]

	Money Earnings per year	Average Weeks Worked	Earnings per Week Employed
Men (over 20)	$1,083	41.3	26.23
Women (over 20)	629	46.4	13.53
Boys (under 20)	406	41.1	9.88
Girls (under 20)	368	43.8	8.40

If we assume that in the full prosperity of the late twenties forty-eight weeks of work would be the norm (a very generous estimate for Montreal) and make a further assumption on the basis of the wage rate index that wages declined by five per cent from 1929 to 1931, the averages for 1928-29 work out to $1,321 for men, $682 for women, $497 for boys, and $423 for girls. These estimates, by including salary earners, do not represent average incomes for the working class. Marsh developed a classification system for wage and salary earners which allows us to examine a more meaningful income picture than is possible through the use of simple averages. In the following table the

AVERAGE ANNUAL INCOMES OF ADULT MALE WAGE AND SALARY EARNERS, MONTREAL — 1928 - 1929

	Income	% of labour force
Managerial	$3438	2.8%
Professional	$2347	4.1%
Commercial	$1972	4.0%
Responsible (Foreman and Overseers)	$1752	4.1%
Clerical	$1336	9.2%
AVERAGE ALL WAGE EARNERS	$1321	
Skilled	$1270	20.6%
Salesmen	$1367	4.1%
Intermediate Service	$1000	4.1%
Semi-skilled	$1000	10.9%
Low-skilled Service	$783	3.4%
Unskilled	$836	29.3%

incomes of eleven categories of wage and salary earners are averaged on the basis of full employment estimates and a five per cent addition to compensate for possible wage cuts.

It is clear that even with the very liberal adjustments made in the above calculations that 47 per cent of all adult male wage earners averaged less than $1,100 per year at full employment and a further 20 per cent earned less than $1,300 per year. Measured against the modest "Typical Expenditures of a Family of Five budget" this means that, even at the peak of prosperity in the late 1920s, the average income for adult male workers in occupations which account for at least 67 per cent of the labour force fell well below the minimum income ($1,590) required to support an average family.

Marsh was deeply concerned with the meaning of the statistics he analysed for 1930-31. Since he had discovered that average annual earnings in Montreal were very close to the median for all urban centres in Canada with populations of more than 15,000, his attempt to estimate family income was extended to cover urban workers in Canada. The following table is unadjusted for full employment as it may be presumed that the relationships are similar. (See page 42.)

Marsh noted that on the average male earnings at maturity were close to $1,200 per year and on the average his family contributed an additional $200 per year.[34] Marsh was using a figure of $1,040 as the minimum necessary for an average Canadian in 1931. This figure was suggested by the Canadian Welfare Council, and was "limited to the barest essentials," but Marsh noted that

To allow a small margin of comfort, better housing and clothing, to say nothing of savings, the minimum standard at least in large cities would have to be $1,500. The average level of white collar and responsible workers' families is at or above this and there are a few representatives of the skilled tradesmen class who can maintain it. But this is not an income which grants any sure access to the amenities of modern civilized life, apart altogether from the wider freedom of education, social intercourse and cultivated leisure. What is often called an "American Standard of Living" enabling a liberal and varied diet, housing accommodation which includes a few domestic labour-saving devices, reasonable provision for health and recreation etc., requires at the most frugal calculation $2,000; and some would put it considerably higher. This is characteristic of only managerial, professional and higher

TYPICAL INCOMES OF OCCUPATIONAL CLASSES IN CANADA –1930-1931

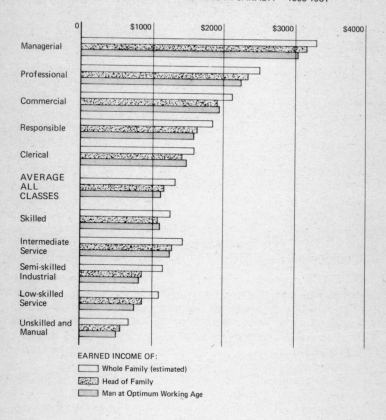

grade commercial and clerical families, the upper fifteen per cent of wage and salary earners; at a generous estimate not more than a quarter of all Canadian families.[35]

Even using the full employment estimates average family incomes for 47 per cent of the Montreal labour force fall well below our poverty line and an additional 25 per cent are on the edge of the $1,590 mark.

During thirty years of great economic growth the urban-industrial working class in Montreal had lived within a culture of poverty, created primarily by subsistence incomes and an absence of job security. The evidence suggests that this pattern held for workers of all ethnic groups though it is clear that French-speaking workers were over-represented in the lowest income categories and badly under-represented in skilled occupations and among foremen. Part of the reason for this ethnic correlation lies in the heavy weight of British-born immigrants in the "skilled" and "responsible" categories[36] but the dominance of English as the language of business must also have played a large part.

Workers of all ethnic origins were caught in the same trap. Wage rates were based on a calculation of the minimum required to recruit a work force. By the 1920s some employers had begun to talk about relating wages to productivity but there were no angels of that sort in Montreal and the labour unions had enough difficulty in keeping the wages of their members in line with increases in the cost of living. R. H. Coats in his study of the cost of living in Canada, published in 1915, observed that wage levels had not kept pace with increases in productivity in the first fifteen years of the century[37] and there is no indication that this pattern was reversed in the next fifteen years. Employers would have to be compelled to alter their views on labour as a commodity to be bought at the lowest possible price and only mass unionization could force the issue.

Chapter 3
Women and Children in the Labour Force

The wages of the Montreal workingman, in the years between 1890 and 1930, remained at the subsistence level, and sometimes dropped below it. That was the central fact of a workingman's life in these years. A succession of booms might be based upon his labour, but he did not share in them. Just about every aspect of the situation of the working class was connected with this fact. One of the most injurious consequences was the hard necessity for children, as well as young unmarried women, to go to work at as early an age as possible. Working class families were thus caught in a classic bind. Since the head of the household normally did not make enough to support his family, his children had to contribute to the family's income through their own labour. Yet the availability on the labour market of large numbers of children and young women helped keep men's wages at the subsistence level.

Large numbers of working class women were "emancipated" from the bondage of unpaid labour at home long before their middle class counterparts won entry into male-dominated high income occupations. There was no need to struggle against an exclusionist policy, since employers were only too happy to provide opportunities for women in the factories, shops, and garment lofts of the city. There was equally strong demand for domestic servants, indeed it might be said that this was the only occupation with a totally elastic demand curve.

Estimates of the number of women in the labour force prior to 1921 can only be rough approximations. Ames' figure of 20 per cent for 1896[1] seems likely to be accurate and the census of 1921, which shows 60,027[2] women employees or 25 per cent of the labour force, fits in with the general view that women were being increasingly drawn into wage employment. The 1931 Census records 85,383[3] women income earners, 25.2 per cent of the gainfully occupied. Between 1901 and 1929 more than one-third of all women employees were engaged in the manufacturing sector. A further third of the total was employed in the service category, mainly domestic service, and the remainder in a variety of occupations which had one common feature – low wages.

The marital status of women wage-earners cannot be clearly ascertained from published Census data. The indications are that married women constituted a small proportion of the manufacturing work force but a considerable percentage of those engaged in domestic work. More than 25 per cent of all women workers in Montreal in 1921 were under twenty-one and 51 per cent were under twenty-five.[4] This heavy preponderance of young women, who it was generally presumed would marry and take up unpaid work in their homes, may account for the widespread indifference to the plight of the female worker. Certainly the factory inspectors, who devoted so much energy to the question of child labour, raised relatively few questions about the wages and working conditions of adult women factory operatives.

Women were linked with children in regulatory legislation and thus received whatever protection rules forbidding their employment in "dangerous or unhealthy occupations" provided. Women could not legally be employed for more than sixty hours a week unless a special permit was obtained for a period "not exceeding six weeks."[5] After 1913 this limit was set at fifty-eight hours and in 1915 textile workers were restricted to fifty-five hours per week.[6] The limit of fifty-five hours was extended to all occupations regulated by the factory inspectors in 1930.

Some women workers were affected by collective bargaining agreements, notably the contract signed by the Amalgamated Clothing Workers in 1924 which obtained the forty-four hour week for union shops.[7] However, the Department of Labour's surveys of *Hours of Labour in Canada* indicate that the norm for women wage earners in the 1920s was fifty-two to fifty-five hours a week.[8] The textile industry continued to treat the maximum as the minimum and hours in the other major women's occupations remained higher than the average for all occupations.

The Quebec Government responded to the generalized concern about women workers that developed during the war by introducing legislation creating a Women's Minimum Wage Commission in 1919. The Act was said to be based on British Columbia legislation and gave the board power to issue minimum wage regulations for various industries. The legislation was a hastily enacted token response to the vague reform sentiment of the day. Louis Guyon did not hesitate to point out that no money had been appropriated to pay for a staff and conse-

Women's lunch room, British Munitions Supply Company Limited, Verdun, 1916-1918.

quently the Commission had "little chance of success."[9] Eight years passed before the legislation was amended and money provided for the Commission.

Gustave Francq, a veteran of the international trade union movement and former leader of the *Parti Ouvrier*, was appointed Chairman. (No women were appointed to the Board.) The first task of the Commission was an attempt to establish a budget for a working woman's living expenses. A number of questionnaires were sent out and the replies indicated that a single woman's living expenses came to somewhere between $10.85 and $19.81 a week. The Commission opted for a minimum of $12.20 a week or $634.40 per year. The rationale for this choice seems to have been that it was close to minimum wages paid by the larger establishments. The Chairman explained that the wide range between minimum and maximum budgets was due to differences about costs of "incidental and frivolous expenditures." There was, he reported, basic agreement that seven dollars a week provided room and board.[10] Eleven dollars and fifty cents a month was the budget for clothing and eleven dollars a month for "sundries." After streetcar fare was deducted, a woman would have twenty-five cents a day left over from which she was presumably to save money for the inevitable winter slowdown or generally to go to hell on.

The first regulation issued by the Commission came into force in 1928. It covered 10,189 working women in thirty-nine textile establishments. Experienced women with more than twenty-four months of employment were to be paid not less than $12.00 for a fifty-five hour week. The Commission noted that "employers had to be convinced that the Commission was not erected to cause them trouble ... or upset their industry" and the Chairman reported that

According to the testimony of employers' representatives the putting into effect of the minimum wage enactment, far from hurting their industry has rather stabilized it, suppressing the unfair competition of a small number of employers.[11]

The Commission's desire not to upset employers continued to be evident in their regulations for the 2,304 women in the boot and shoe industry who were guaranteed a minimum of $12.50 a week after two years.[12] In 1929 the Commission tackled the needle trades, which employed 9,510 women workers. Of this total, slightly less than half were categorized as young and inexperienced workers, who averaged weekly earnings of $8.37, while 5,431 women with advanced skills averaged $16.95 a week. The new min-

47

imum for the first category was set at $8.50 and for the second group at $12.50.[13] The tobacco industry reported 1,986 women in the inexperienced category who earned average wages of $9.28 a week and 1,353 women who averaged $15.67. The new minimums for the two groups were set at $8.50 and $12.50.[14]

Clearly the Women's Minimum Wage Commission, despite the presence of trade unionists on its staff, operated within the traditions of North American regulatory boards. The purpose of regulation was to promote stability and legitimatize the policies of the larger, more efficient firms. Minimum wage laws were not intended to raise overall wage rates; indeed in practice their effect was rather to provide a justification for low wages.

The factory inspectors did not entirely ignore women workers. After 1896 female factory inspectors were charged with special responsibility for occupations employing large numbers of women and some pressure was exerted with regard to the conditions of the work place. The main concerns were separate toilets for women, lunchrooms, and factory cleanliness. The factory inspectors were equally concerned with protecting the morals of working women – Madame Louise Provencher and her colleague, Louisa King, made frequent reference to such matters. In 1897 Madame Provencher expressed her fears about the mingling of the sexes in workshops and observed:

> Some masters conduct their establishments in a manner worthy of all praise . . . the workwomen are separated from the men and silence is strictly enforced. This is generally preferable not only for the good of young girls but for the benefit of the master.[15]

Madame Provencher's concern with moral standards led her to make frequent observations on the conduct of factory girls. She expressed concern, in one of her reports, about "a very young woman reading Lamartine's *Jocelyn*." "Who," she asked, "had placed in her hands a book so little suited to her in every respect?"[16] On another occasion, Madame Provencher urged that "every working girl caught in using certain words or in raising improper questions should be immediately discharged."[17] Louisa King, who was constantly pressing for improved ventilation, cleanliness, lunchrooms, and, after 1903, seats for shopgirls "who had to stand from eight in the morning until six at night," was well satisfied with the effects of her work. In 1904 she described her role in the following terms:

Like bounteous dew falling noiselessly on thirsty plants and reviving them, like the sun's rays that spread joy and life wherever they shine, thus does the inspectress fulfill her mission.[18]

Louis Guyon's views on women wage earners were typical of what passed for wisdom among most students of social questions. They are quoted at length because they are representative.

Woman's work, outside of her home, is one of the sad novelties of the modern world; it is a true social heresy. Woman, outside of her home, appears to us as a being out of place, a woman without a country. Formerly, in primitive society woman hardly differed from man; engaged in the hardest work, by a phenomenon of adaptation she assumed the roughness and the temperament of men. In civilized societies, especially in christian societies, education and culture restore the woman to her sex and develop her aptitudes as a woman.

The economic fatalities of the present time seem to have taken that feminine feature away from woman, in general. Having to work like a man, and very often with men, in the promiscuousness of the factory or workshop to earn her bread as man does, she claims her due; such is feminism.

"Such singularities are due to a fleeting crisis, the social crisis of the present day."

A learned sociologue says: "On the day when, as formerly, the woman possesses her home – and society must restore it to her, if it does not wish to degenerate – on the day when she finds in her home her daily bread of security for the morrow, then will the feminine question be solved to the extent of three fourths if not entirely."

Happily we have not, in our country, the problem of the married woman in workshops and factories, with a few rare exceptions, not enough numerous, it seems to me, to call for the introduction of a special Act in our Statutes.

The presence of the few married women we find in our factories is in most instances due to the desertion of their husbands.

With regard to the work of single women, it would be wonderful if society could, some day or another, find an economic formula capable of doing away with it, but economic exigences control and dominate all. Rivers do not run back to their sources. Nevertheless, society requires, and with reason, that the work of woman be surrounded with all the protection and consideration due to her sex; the same applies to children.[19]

Guyon did not specify just what "protection and consideration" was owed to women because of their sex but presumably he thought existing labour laws accomplished what was needed.

* * *

The complacency which marked official attitudes towards women workers was not present, in the same degree, where children were concerned. The problem of children in the work force tugged more compellingly at society's conscience. And a problem there was. Most North American cities had their share of messenger boys, delivery boys and newsboys, but in Montreal children were a major part of the work force. This was not solely because the low wages of their fathers forced children to seek employment, but also because Montreal, like a number of other cities on the continent, had the kinds of industries in which there was a demand for unskilled labour performing routine tasks.

John Spargo, the author of the most thorough survey of child labour practices in the United States in the early years of the twentieth century, noted that the textile industries "rank first in the enslavement of children."[20] The textiles industry was a major employer in Montreal's economy and child labour was as common in the mills of the city as it was in the mill towns of New England. The tobacco, glass, food processing and garment industries were also high on the list of consumers of child labour and all of these activities were important in the economy of Montreal.

No accurate estimate of the extent of child labour in Montreal can be put forward. H. B. Ames reported that about 4 per cent of the labour force in his "City Below the Hill" was composed of children[21] and this is very close to the figure for the manufacturing sector reported in the 1901 census. However, Ames did not specify the age which marked off "children" from "lads" and the census data was developed from returns provided by manufacturers – not the best source for accurate information. Spargo's investigation indicated that the 1900 U.S. Census figure of 1.7 million children under sixteen in the labour force was completely inaccurate and he estimated that there were 2.2 million children under *fifteen* years of age at work.[22]

The problem of child labour in Montreal can best be approached by describing the campaign to end child labour waged by Louis Guyon, the Chief Factory Inspector for the province. Guyon was not the only crusader for the abolition of child labour but he and his associates were the ones who best knew the scope of the problem and knew it from direct experience.

The Industrial Establishments Act had set the minimum age for factory workers at twelve for boys and fourteen for girls. Proof of age in the form of a certificate signed by the parents was required and the inspectors were supposed to check those certificates on their yearly visits. In 1897 Guyon noted, with the ironic understatement which marked so many of his comments, that

> There have been very few infractions to note in regard to the employment of children under age; the limit of 12 years for boys being so low that there is hardly any desire to employ them younger . . . .[23]

It may be that as long as the legal age of entry for boys was twelve relatively few were illegally employed in factories, but girls under the age of fourteen were often discovered at work. Madame Louise Provencher, who was appointed to the inspectorate in 1898 with special responsibility for factories employing women and children, noted in her 1901 report that

> This year I sent away from factories five little girls under fourteen . . . . It frequently happens that girls and boys seem to be much younger than they really are according to the certificates signed by their parents.[24]

Her colleague, Louisa King, reported that she had found no instances of violation of the law but was "painfully impressed by the puny and delicate appearance of child workers in factories."[25] Over the next few years, Louisa King returned to the theme that people were misled as to the age of children in factories. "I myself" she wrote in 1905, "am sometimes still deceived as to the age of children owing to their occasionally slight appearance."[26] Three years later she cautioned that "people who tried to judge the age of working children by appearance will often be mistaken. The parents are small, the children are smaller – what are the future generations going to be like?"[27]

If the factory inspectors were in doubt as to the extent of violations of the existing age limits they were all in agreement as to the need for raising the minimum age for boys to fourteen. Their reports also agree that the problem of child labour was steadily growing as the economy prospered. Not only did they locate many more underage children in their tours of inspection but they reported that the demand for children capable of producing a certificate claiming they were of age was "very great."[28] In his 1898 Report, Guyon had written,

> Thanks to the wonderful progress of mechanics, the supporting of the adult by the child in the manufacture of many articles has been made possible,[29]

and in 1903 he noted that strikes in the tobacco industry had led to "mechanization and increased employment of children."[30]

Child labour in the industrial establishments checked by the inspectors was only a part of the problem. The law made no provision for the supervision of home workshops, retail stores or the street trades. In 1903 Guyon complained:

> It must not be forgotten that the employees in the majority of our shops are chiefly children ... shops should have been brought under the Industrial Establishment Act so as to allow our intervention.[31]

No action was taken on this problem or on the "thousands of working children ... errand boys and newsboys," that Guyon reported could be seen "shivering on the street until eleven o'clock at night."[32]

From the beginning Louis Guyon tied his campaign to limit child labour to the need for providing children with a basic education. In 1897 he argued that

> Little boys of 12 and little girls of 14 who have been only a short time at school soon forget what they have learned. At the end of a year there remains very frequently not a trace of those indispensible elements [reading and writing] acquired with so much effort.[33]

After his appointment as Chief Factory Inspector, he consistently pressed for a literacy requirement for working children.

> I am convinced that our law is doomed to barrenness as a measure of social reform so long as age alone furnishes the passport of admission to the factory. Both in Europe and the United States all labour laws are based on elementary education . . . .[34]

In 1901 he described himself as a "convinced advocate of 'admitting' children to factories on the basis of education and physical condition" and reported that he had personally investigated one of our large cotton mills. . . . out of 65 girls, 13 were illiterate, 18 wrote with difficulty. Out of 65 boys, 21 were illiterate and 11 could hardly sign their names.[35]

The Provincial Government responded to Guyon's campaign and the publicity it attracted by raising the minimum age for boys to thirteen in 1903. Then in 1907 the Quebec Legislature amended the I.E.A., setting the minimum age at fourteen and including a test of literacy for fourteen year olds entering the factory work force. An additional clause provided for compulsory attendance at night school for fourteen to sixteen year olds who were unable to satisfy the inspectors that they could read and wirte.
Guyon was far from satisfied.

The obligation for children between 14 and 16 to be literate or attend night school is a very difficult one to fulfill . . . in the first place because, in many cases, there are no night schools, and at best for boys only . . . .
If I have fully seized the legislators' idea, the obligation for children to attend night school could only have been preparatory to a general law compelling children between 14 and 16 to fulfill the requirements regarding elementary education. Is it very practical to compel a child fatigued by ten hours of assiduous labour to spend even an hour and a half at school?
A great many employers have assured me that they would favour a regulation compelling parents to keep their children at school.[36]

Guyon's question about the practicality of night school for children who had worked a ten hour day went unanswered, but the inspectors kept asking. A Miss R. Barry, who was appointed to the inspectorate in 1908, wrote that,

. . . many children, especially boys, can hardly spell and cannot write. I told them that they must attend night school but I feel some repugnance in pressing. . . . Is it not cruel?[37]

Guyon was already developing a new flank attack in recommending that the literacy test be replaced by a school principal's certificate of elementary education. Year after year Guyon argued for this reform. In 1913 he wrote,

In many countries child labour has ceased to be a problem it formerly was because every boy and girl is obliged to hand to his employer, with his age certificate, his school attendance book. . . . In the City of Montreal, for the cotton spinning industry alone, it takes at least a week to examine the children regarding their age or degree of education.[38]

The proposal came too close to advocating compulsory education for the members of the Legislative Assembly. In 1918 the government decided to institute a general examination of literacy for fourteen to sixteen year olds and to insist upon successful completion of the exam or compulsory attendance at night school. The first examination held under this system in 1920 involved the testing of 6,912 fourteen to sixteen year olds and of these, 3,081 were judged deficient. The Report noted,

> some of them who could write, in a fairly good hand, their names, their addresses and the name of the company employing them, could read only hesitatingly while others who could read very well could write only with difficulty.[39]

Four per cent of the girls tested and eight per cent of the boys were judged to be completely illiterate, though the percentages among immigrant children were "a little higher." The examination had involved only a small fraction of the children in the work force. The Labour Department estimated that there were "between eleven and twelve thousand children between 14 and 16 working in Montreal alone, not to speak of the industrial suburbs."[40]

Guyon and his associates were convinced that the "dearth of operatives" available in the latter stages of the war had added immeasurably to the problem of child labour. In 1916 he wrote that "child labour remains the same unsolvable problem we have encountered . . . since 1888."[41] The following year his report included two anecdotes, one of a mother who pleaded with him not to send her child away and a second story of "a boy, ten years old who had been sent to the factory by his father and had his arm torn off."[42] Guyon's experience led him to view child labour as an unmitigated disaster and he hoped the new system of compulsory registration would act as an incentive to keep children in school.

In 1921 seven thousand additional children under the age of sixteen were registered. Guyon's report reiterated the old theme about child workers outside the purview of the inspectors. "A good number of children 14 and under will escape all control" he wrote, "because our inspectors have not always jurisdiction in the places where they are employed." In addition,

> There have come to the bureau a good many widows with

children and more than a hundred women whose husbands were ill .... All of these mothers asked for a special permit for illiterate children or those underage. After investigation in every *bona fide* case certificates were issued for the holiday season.[43]

Guyon expressed the hope that such children would return to school at the end of the summer but he was disturbed about the difficulties in enforcing the new law with his limited staff. "It would be advisable," he wrote,

> to confide the examination of children to the school authorities .... The Department can always, at its discretion, compel the child to follow night school courses but experience has shown that almost insurmountable difficulties would be met in effectually controlling the presence of scholars at school.... [44]

He explained that many children went to a night school and registered, acquired the necessary form and then never returned.

Between 1922 and 1929 more than two thousand children were registered by the Montreal Labour Bureau in each year.[45] Given the limited scope of the I.E.A. and the problem of adequate enforcement, it is not possible even to guess what percentage of the total number of fourteen and fifteen year olds in the work force that this number represents but it would be reasonable to conclude that large numbers of children under fifteen years of age continued to enter the labour force.

Louis Guyon had become Deputy Minister of Labour in 1919 and his new position gradually removed him from daily contact with factory conditions. After 1923 the Labour Department stopped publishing detailed reports from factory inspectors and Guyon's summaries became vague and self-congratulatory. In 1925 he wrote that our "code of labour laws amply meets present requirements."[46] He believed that proposed amendments to the Workman's Compensation Act and the creation of a board under the Women's Minimum Wage Act would put Quebec on a par with other provinces and fulfill his grand design. Two years later he returned to the child labour question with the odd statement that, "the story of children ten to twelve years old in factories is dead."[47] No doubt it was, but Guyon had fought that battle twenty-five years previously. Children between the ages of fourteen and sixteen were still entering the factory labour force in large numbers throughout the 1920s and most of them were employed in dead-end jobs at miserable wages. It should be noted in this connection that a very small percentage of children were employed as apprentices. In 1921 only 361 children fifteen years of age and younger were recorded as apprentices out of a census total of 5,732 such children at work in Montreal.[48]

In addition to their attempts to eliminate child labour, the factory inspectors had tried to effect changes in the conditions under which children were employed. The only special provisions in the law regarding the conditions under which children worked were a statement in the I.E.A. forbidding their employment in dangerous or unhealthy occupations (a vague and therefore unenforceable restriction) and a clause limiting their hours of work to a maximum of ten a day "unless a special permit was obtained for a period not exceeding six weeks." It was not until 1911 that the legal limit of the working week for children and women was reduced to fifty-eight hours.[49] Two years later the hours of women and children in textile mills were set at fifty-five hours per week but this rule was not extended to other occupations until 1930.[50] The textile industry was singled out because it was the major consumer of child labour and because conditions in the mills were "toilsome and depressing."[51]

There was some debate among the factory inspectors as to the physical surroundings in which children laboured. Madame Provencher's tours moved her to write that the "wretched use of childhood is especially painful and one must be hardhearted not to be moved at the sight of it."[52] James Mitchell, however, was sufficiently hard-hearted to argue, with unintentional irony, that

Statements regarding conditions under which children work in textile mills should be received with caution. Many are much more comfortable, especially during the winter months than in their own homes.[53]

Apart from the very limited changes in the legal limit of the work week, children were granted no special privileges in the work world. Moreover, the campaign to ensure a degree of literacy among young workers was a failure. All of the available statistical evidence suggests that between 1901 and 1921 the number of working children between ten and fifteen years of age increased both absolutely and as a proportion of the age group.[54] This was evident to the factory inspectors in Montreal who were particularly struck by the increase in child labour during the war. It is likely that the proportion of the age group from ten to fifteen years at work declined slightly in the 1920s but the 1931 Census shows 3,730 children fifteen and under at work so the problem was far from resolved.

Chapter 4

Formal Education and the Working Class

Legislation to prevent underage working class children from entering the labour force was ineffective; so was the nostrum of a literacy test as a means of raising the educational level of children already at work. The school system had, at best, only a few years to work miracles with such children before hard economic realities forced them to go to work, but even here the working class child's educational opportunities were limited.

The primary purpose of this chapter is to evaluate the educational opportunities available to working class children in Montreal. The underlying assumption of the analysis is that all children in an urban-industrial society benefit from formal instruction in the basic skills of reading and writing and that they also benefit from the school experience in other ways. No attempt is made here to argue that there is a clear relationship between years of schooling and income or occupation. Education was no doubt a contributing factor to the pattern of individual careers but for the mass of the population, the structure of the economy established rigid occupational limitations. Our concern with education is therefore limited to the question of why working class children were so often deprived of the opportunity to attend school during the short period of their lives when they were not in demand as wage earners.

In theory the public educational system which existed in Montreal at the turn of the century was organized to meet the objective of universal primary education.[1] In practice access to the neighbourhood primary school was severely restricted in many parts of the city and the quality of schools varied tremendously. Much the same could be said about schools in any large, rapidly expanding North American city but the available comparative evidence suggests that these problems were particularly acute in Montreal. Before proceeding to an examination of the problem of school attendance in Montreal, it seems necessary to deal with some of the assumptions about education in French Canada which cloud the issue of free access to schooling.

Quebec's education system has long been singled out as a crucial variable in historical, sociological, and journalistic investigations into the "backwardness" or "retardation" of French Canadian society. Such studies have usually made a number of assumptions about education which seem questionable. No empirical evidence has ever established that "Catholic" education *per se* or education provided by members of religious orders is inferior or superior to "Protestant" or "state" education. A specific school may provide a "better" environment for an individual child but anyone who goes beyond that generalization is simply expressing his or her preference.

Reference is frequently made to the alleged deficiencies in "scientific" and "practical" education in the schools of French Canada. It should first be noted that for the overwhelming majority of the population education meant elementary school until very recently. The amount of "scientific" work done in the elementary schools of any part of North America until the 1950s was, of course, minimal. Even at the secondary school level curriculums from the early twentieth century suggest that such schools were designed to provide a "classical" rather than "scientific" education. French Canadian secondary education was at least as "practical" or vocational as that in English Canada. One third of the students registered in classical colleges were in the Commercial Course[2] and, as the Royal Commission on Industrial Training and Technical Education noted, Montreal in 1913 had one of the "finest" technical schools in North America.[3] The English language was assigned an important place in French language schools and it was taught as the language of commerce not Shakespeare.[4]

The basis of common assumptions about the greater practicality of education in English-speaking Canada seems to be related to the higher proportion of skilled and white collar workers in the English-speaking population. To the degree that this was not due to a language-race barrier, the cause is surely to be found in English Canada's ability to draw on a reserve of educated and skilled labour from the United Kingdom and the United States[5] rather than the influence of the elitist and restrictive educational systems of English-speaking Canada.

In the early years of the twentieth century a number of French Canadians were well aware of the role that immigration played in reinforcing Anglophone dominance of skilled trades and that is why so much energy was directed towards the creation of the École des Hautes Études Commerciales and technical schools.[6]

In recent years, French Canadian historians have tended to

adopt the kind of criticism of Quebec's education system which used to be put forward by the more rabid Francophobes in English-speaking Canada. Michel Brunet, for example, sees the "Church" and its lay supporters as a monolithic and reactionary force in Quebec education. Writing of the turn of the century period he accuses "L'épiscopat, appuyé par les groupes traditionalistes et conservateurs," of responsibility for retarding Quebec's educational development.

> Au nom de l'anti-maçonnisme et de l'anti-étatisme ou au nom de la religion, les principaux dirigeants de la collectivité défendirent aveuglément le *statu quo*. Ils s'opposèrent à l'école obligatoire, à l'uniformisation des manuels scolaires, à la fondation de l'École des Hautes Études Commerciales, à la centralisation scolaire dans des villes, à la suppression des écoles de rang, à la création d'écoles spécialisées dirigées par l'État, à une meilleure organisation de la profession enseignante, à la réforme du Départment d l'Instruction publique, etc. [7]

Brunet's charges, which are typical of such criticism, contain an element of truth but the overall impression is misleading. Throughout the first two decades of the century and intermittently thereafter, an acrimonious debate between supporters of church controlled and state controlled schools did poison the atmosphere of French Canadian society. This debate, however, was largely concocted out of the ideological preoccupations of French Canadian intellectuals, not from an analysis of the strengths and weaknesses of the school system.

The chief critic of the province's education system in the early years of the twentieth century was Godfroy Langlois, a self-styled *vieux rouge*.[8] Langlois became the spokesman for the *Ligue de l'Enseignement,* an organization which claimed to be interested in promoting dialogue on basic questions such as teachers' salaries, medical inspection of school children, uniform school tests, and compulsory education.[9] Langlois was a man of remarkable energy and vision, but his anti-clerical views, his support for the creation of a Ministry of Education, and his personal commitment to a compulsory attendance law meant that the *Ligue* would be regarded as a pressure group campaigning for an end to church controlled education rather than as a forum for the discussion of educational reform. The very choice of the name *Ligue de l'Enseignement* was deliberately provocative. The identical name had been adopted in France for an organization which was popularly understood to have been responsible for banishing religion from the schools of France.

The reaction to Langlois' campaign was certainly excessive if predictable. Cries of "la conspiration maçonnique" were accompanied by elaborate and exaggerated portrayals of Quebec's schools as the best in North America. *L'Enseignement Primaire,* the official organ of the Council of Public Instruction, published statistical and philosophical justifications of the Quebec system and numerous clerical and lay activists jumped to the defence of Catholic education.[10] The important point, however, is what happened, not what the intellectuals fought about. Taking Brunet's list as a starting point it should be noted that the École des Hautes Études Commerciales was established, school centralization begun,[11] specialized schools like the Montreal Technical Institute created, and Normal Schools built in many centres of the province. Overall state control of education and a compulsory attendance law did not develop until 1962 and 1942 respectively, but there was no necessary connection between these measures and an adequate education system.

When Lomer Gouin became Premier of Quebec in 1905 he disavowed his earlier interest in the *Ligue* and after a meeting with the Archbishop of Montreal declared

> nous ne voulons ni détruire ni révolutionner: nous voulons améliorer et fortifier. Nos lois scolaires sont aussi bonnes que nous puissions les désirer, et le gouvernement n'a pas l'intention d'en changer les principes. On a parlé d'un ministère de l'instruction publique. Cette suggestion a été faite de bonne foi, je n'en doute pas. Mais pourquoi recommencer des discussions et faire revivre des malaises qui stériliseront les efforts que tous les hommes de bonne volonté sont disposés a faire pour le progrès de l'enseignement en cette province.[12]

The Gouin administration did attempt to "améliorer et fortifier" education in Quebec. Its efforts were no doubt only partially successful but the chief constraints on the provincial government and the local school commissions were not ideological in the traditional sense. The real constraint was financial, which was of course the product of a more profound, if less conscious ideology.

The fundamental weakness of the City's education system was the inability of the schools to retain children beyond the third or fourth year of elementary education. Enrolment in the first three years of school, encompassing children between the ages of six and eleven, was generally at a high level but the later grades were very sparsely attended. The Montreal Catholic School Commission published a partial breakdown of its enrolment in fourteen elementary schools in 1905. The number of pupils in first year was 3,442, in the fourth year there were only 1,118, and in the fifth year just 426 students were registered. The average age in the fifth year was thirteen. The M.C.S.C. published this breakdown in order to justify its reduction of monthly fees. "The object in reducing monthly fees," the Commissioners noted, "is to induce students to continue at school until they shall have obtained the certificate for the elementary and model course" (seven years).[13]

The most systematic investigation of school attendance statistics for Montreal was undertaken by a committee of the Provincial Association of Protestant Teachers in 1918.[14] Their *Report* was designed as a "propagandist activity" for the enactment of a compulsory school attendance law. The standard argument used against compulsory education in Quebec was that the province's school attendance statistics compared favourably with those of provinces with compulsory education so there was no need for a new law. The committee questioned the accuracy of the province's overall statistics and compiled enrolment statistics for Montreal schools for the year 1916-17 which indicated that the pattern observed in 1905 had persisted.

	Kindergarten	1	2	3	4	5
Montreal R. C. Schools	–	25,792	13,755	9,547	5,979	2,848
Montreal Protestant Schools	1,187	4,197	3,567	3,502	3,195	2,761
	6	7	8	9	10	11
Montreal R. C. Schools	1,737	1,019	560	–	–	–
Montreal Protestant Schools	1,941	1,243	610	392	278	149

The *Report* noted that,

There are a few thousand of the children of the wealthy who were enrolled elsewhere – a few Protestant children in private schools and some Catholic girls in nunneries and boys in Classical Colleges. But the above figures represent the enrolment of the children of the masses. . . .

Your Committee asks the people of Montreal to consider carefully all that it means to the future welfare of their city when, of all the children of the Public and high schools, there are only 19,627 or 23.2% of the total enrolment beyond the most elementary stages. In Toronto, Ottawa and New York the proportions were respectively 33% (in 1916), 37% (in 1917), and 44% (in 1913). Surely free education without compulsion has not solved the problem of attendance in Montreal.[15]

The Committee's confidence that a compulsory education law would solve the problem of school attendance in Montreal was somewhat naive. A far more basic problem, the financing of public education, had to be tackled before adequate accommodation for even the existing student population could be achieved. It is the organization and financing of public education in Montreal which must be examined if the pattern of school attendance for children under fourteen is to be understood.

The public education system in Montreal was divided into two broad categories, Protestant and Catholic. A number of distinct school boards existed within the metropolitan area at the turn of the century but their general practices were similar to the Catholic and Protestant School Commissions of Montreal. Commissioners were appointed, three by the Quebec Government on the advice of the Superintendent of Public Instruction, three by City Council, and in the case of the Catholic Commission three additional members from the clergy selected by the Archbishop of Montreal.

The Commissions were incorporated bodies charged with the construction, maintenance, staffing, and operation of public schools. Finances were obtained primarily from property taxes paid by the proprietors of real estate. Four tax panels existed, one for Catholic ratepayers, one for Protestants, a third "neutral panel" consisting of corporate ratepayers plus persons who were neither Catholic nor Protestant, and a fourth panel representing religious, charitable, educational, and government property which was tax exempt. Proceeds from the neutral panel were divided according to the percentage of the population of each faith.[16] In addition to municipal property taxes the boards received small grants from the provincial government and collected fees from students.

The net result of the financial arrangement was the provision of relatively adequate sums of money for the Protestant public schools and a disastrously low level of financing for Roman Catholic public education. Supporters of the status quo argued that the extensive network of subsidized private Roman Catholic schools made up for the differences in municipal tax support. There was some truth in this argument from a purely financial point of view, but subsidized private schools had little impact on the majority of the working class population who had to send their children to the overcrowded and impoverished Catholic public schools.

The non-Catholic population constituted less than 25 per cent of the City's population between 1897 and 1910 yet in those years the Protestant School Commission received roughly the same amount of municipal school tax as the Catholic Board. For example, in 1905-06 the Protestant Board with 10,991 pupils received $261,060 in municipal taxes while the Catholic public schools received $232,968 for the support of 20,709 students. Part of this wide differential is made up when the $99,842 contribution of the subsidized private Roman Catholic schools is added to the Catholic total but even then the discrepancy is a large one.[17] As a consequence of this privileged position, the Protestant Board was able to pay its teachers nearly double the salary paid to Catholic teachers as well as creating a number of kindergarten classes in most of its schools.[18] Protestant schools were also generally better equipped in terms of art rooms, gymnasiums, etc.

It may be thought that the large number of teachers belonging to religious orders in the Catholic schools represented an additional subsidy but in fact such teachers cost the board rather more than lay teachers. The Board's contract with the Christian Brothers called for the payment of $500 per teacher and the contracts with female religious orders involved an expenditure of $350 per teacher. Lay male teachers received salaries of $600 per year but there were only a handful of them. Female lay teachers were paid an average of $300 in 1915.[19]

If the Protestant community was relatively better endowed, its tax resources were still inadequate. The Protestant Committee of the Council of Public Instruction launched a campaign in 1897 to have the taxes paid into the neutral panel divided on the basis of the professed religion of the directors of each corporation. Such a change would have destroyed the financial basis of the Montreal Catholic School Commission and its Commissioners entered a strong protest. In a "Memoir on the Division of the School Tax in Montreal" they developed a vigorous counter attack. The Memoir is quoted in full below because in both tone and content it presents a picture of French Canadian Catholic education which is too little known.

The law on public instruction, 8 Vict., ch. 41, s. 42, decreed what follows: "And be it enacted, that in the said cities (Quebec and Montreal) no rate shall be levied for the schools, but the treasurer of each City shall pay out of the funds thereof to the said boards of Commissioners, and in proportion to the population of the religious belief represented by them, a sum equal to that coming to such city from the common school fund," etc., etc.

This law continued in force until 1869, when a tax was imposed for the support of the Montreal schools.

At this time Catholics maintained, that the proceeds of the tax ought to be divided as before, according to the population; the Protestants maintained the contrary, and after a lively and lengthy debate, for political reasons which it is difficult to appreciate today, the two parties came to the understanding which is expressed in 32 Vict., chap. 16, s. 29.

If today, the Protestants wish to break the agreement of 1869, by demanding that the tax coming from corporations or from incorporated societies be divided, according to the religious belief of the owners of the capital, we shall take up the question *ab ovo* and we shall maintain anew that the school tax ought to be divided according to the school population.

Let us lay down the principle that public instruction is a benefit to society, and we arrive logically at the conclusion that all children have an equal right to the benefits of elementary education.

As to superior instruction, those who are favored with the goods of fortune can obtain it, according to their means and their intelligence, in the institutions which are supported by a tax imposed on property.

The tax for the support of primary instruction is imposed on property, but in reality, paid by the occupant.

Today, Protestants who number scarcely a quarter of the population of Montreal receive as much as Catholics who number three-quarters.

Some years hence, it is not impossible that three-quarters of the property may belong to Protestants, in which case we shall have three-fourths of the children to educate and one-fourth of the school tax.

With this revenue, quite contrary to justice and equity, Catholics see themselves absolutely unable to educate their children, and yet it is they who in reality pay the tax. The only means of avoiding this sad inconvenience, so grave for Catholics and so dangerous for Protestants, is the division of the tax according to the school population.

We say, so grave for Catholics, since they would be consigned to ignorance, and, so dangerous for Protestants, since the more property one has, the more is one interested in keeping the population educated and moral.

The principle of separate schools is not opposed by any means to this division.

The law recognizes at Montreal a school commission for the government of Catholic schools and a school commission for the government of Protestant schools; each of these commissions will receive from the proceeds of the tax its just share, according to the number of children to be educated, and, as each religious denomination has a committee of the Council of Public Instruction under which education is placed, the taxpayers can continue to send their children to the schools of their religious belief, without any inconvenience.

The two school commisions agree in saying that their revenues are insufficient to maintain their schools on a perfectly efficient footing.

On the other hand, people tell us we must not think of augmenting the rate of the school tax.

Nevertheless the schools must be maintained.

The Catholics of Montreal find themselves in one of the most trying positions that it is possible to imagine; their revenues are limited to the sum produced by the property tax, which is fixed at ¼ of a cent on the dollar, but their obligations are unlimited, the population increases every year by a greater number of families coming from all parts, the schools of the ancient parishes become too small; in the new they are obliged to place the classes in the basement of temporary churches, and money fails even to pay the meagre salary of the teachers.

To obviate this sad state of things, we propose the division of the tax according to the school population, or, we shall demand of the Government the power to prepare in due time, the budget for the school year next following, and the obligation on the part of the corporation of levying in advance a tax sufficient to meet this budget; which is the way regulated in most of the cities of the United States, and also, they tell us, in the Province of Ontario.[20]

The memoir provides evidence of the strong sense of grievance which the Catholic school commissioners entertained towards the existing tax system. It also points to the real crisis in elementary education which the city was beginning to experience by the turn of the century. The school tax controversy of 1897-1900 was "resolved" by maintaining the status quo but the problem of inadequate school facilities continued to plague both boards throughout the first thirty years of the twentieth century. By 1903 the Catholic Commission had built two new schools in working class areas but the Board was still hard pressed to find space. The Commissioners reported in 1903-04 that,

> Notwithstanding the large number of pupils received into our schools complaint has been made that many children are prevented from receiving instruction on account of want of room in the present school.[21]

Two years later the M.C.S.C. reported that

> provision remains to be made to meet the pressing needs of existing schools when the number seeking admission are becoming daily more and more numerous and to provide schools for certain localities which have none but greatly need them.[22]

The problem of too few schools and too little room was also confronting the Protestant Board. In 1907-08 its Commissioners alluded to the current debate over compulsory education.

> While school boards in other cities in America and Europe are engaged with the enforcement of compulsory school attendance the Protestant School Board of Montreal struggles with the problem of providing sufficient accommodation for the pupils who voluntarily attend. . . . [23]

The pressure of numbers on the existing school facilities added to the problems of health and safety in the older school buildings. The Provincial Board of Health was particularly concerned about the absence of fire escapes in the schools of Metropolitan Montreal. Frequent reference was also made by health inspectors to overcrowding and poor ventilation. When City Health officials began periodic medical inspection of school children their reports revealed the existence of an enormous public health problem, but as the Protestant Board noted all that could be done was to send children home. "Medical inspection," the Board declared, "is of little or no value in itself except to demonstrate the need for more inspection and education and possibly for compulsory or at least free treatment."[24] The Protestant Board was able to afford the appointment of two nurses from the Victorian Order of Nurses but the Catholic schools were denied the service of school nurses until the Municipal Health Department developed a token school nurse service in the 1920s.

Both Boards constantly returned to the theme of too little space in too few schools. The Protestant Board came under particular pressure in the ten years before the war as a result of heavy Jewish immigration to the city. By 1915 43 per cent of all its students were of the Jewish faith and the Board's enrolment, 22,606, was double the 1905 figure.[25] Eighteen new schools had been constructed since 1905 but the Board noted in its 1915 Report that "demands for accommodation are so insistent that temporary classrooms have been erected."[26]

A study of the educational facilities available to the "foreign element"* in Montreal, prepared in 1915, concluded that there were as many as 3,600 Russian, Polish, Hungarian, Bulgarian, Romanian, Ruthenian, Greek, and Syrian children of school age in the city who as members of the Greek or Russian Orthodox Church had no legal right to attend school. The *Report* concluded that "practically none of them are in school" and suggested that "the total number of foreign children in Montreal without regular school facilities would be about 5,000."[27] Gradually the children of the "foreign element" were admitted to Protestant public schools where the religious situation was more flexible and where in any case the large Jewish student body had already paved the way towards a more secularized education than was possible in the Roman Catholic schools.

The problem of inadequate elementary school facilities remained unresolved throughout the "prosperous" 1920s. The M.C.S.C. repeatedly requested money for the construction of new schools. The Board's Financial Report for 1926-1927 noted that the population of the city was spreading north-east and south-west and that

> the need of new schools has made itself immediately felt in these new districts. In face of the dilemma of letting the children run the streets and refusing them schooling or of constructing schools what will be done?[28]

The answer was "very little." Public education for Catholics of both the French and English-speaking communities existed in an atmosphere of financial stringency until the 1950s. Protestant

---

* Jews were, for the purposes of the inquiry, not counted among the "foreign element." Their legal right to attend Protestant schools had been firmly established in 1903.

public education seems to have weathered the crisis of numbers and during the 1920s the Board was able to concentrate on expanding secondary education.

Public secondary education for Catholics was long delayed because of financial stringency. Before the 1920s only Plateau Academy for boys and Marchand Academy for girls offered a two-year post-primary course. The M.C.S.C. had the authority to establish secondary schools (écoles primaires supérieures) from 1911 on[29] but it was not until 1921 that Plateau offered a senior high school year and not until 1922 that the École St-Louis opened as what *Le Canada* called "un High School Canadien Français."[30] English-speaking Catholics were somewhat better served than French Canadians but their resources were meagre indeed when compared to the high schools of the Protestant system.

The financial squeeze on public education was fought most systematically by the Protestant School Board and its supporters. The Board had turned away from its ill-advised attempt to gain an even more preferential split of the tax dollar and instead sought a general tax increase. A carefully researched brief, *The Financial Conditions and Needs of the Protestant Schools of Montreal*,[31] published in 1908, was instrumental in persuading the provincial government to impose a special tax of one mill on the Protestant and Neutral tax panels. Catholic public schools received 75 per cent of the additional revenue from the Neutral panel but the per student increase was much greater for the Protestant Board which received the entire sum collected from the Protestant panel. Further increases were obtained in 1919, 1921, and 1924 and then in 1925 a Protestant Central School Board with the power to collect a uniform school tax from all municipalities on the Island of Montreal was created. The rate after 1924 was ten mills on the Protestant panel and twelve mills on the Neutral panel.[32]

The tax rate on the Catholic panel was raised to seven mills by 1921 but it remained at that level throughout the remainder of the decade.[33] The consequence of this was that the M.C.S.C. received $45.00 in municipal tax support for each student enrolled while the Protestant schools of the Island obtained $87.00 per student. If the Catholic mill rate had been raised to the Protestant level there would have been an additional $8.00 per student available to the Catholic Board.[34]

These calculations refer only to public education. It may be that a detailed analysis of the costs of classical colleges and other private Catholic institutions would show that overall expenditures on education were more proportionate to the percentage of the population of each religious faith.[35] If this was the case its significance for the mass of the Catholic population of Montreal was limited. Classical colleges were designed to form a civil and religious elite, not to promote general access to education.

The financial problems of the Montreal Catholic School Commission resulted in a school system staffed by poorly paid teachers who worked in crowded, inadequate schools. The schools lacked such amenities as kindergartens, manual training rooms, and gymnasiums, not because the Commission or the teachers weren't interested in educational innovation but because there was no money. How can the debate over compulsory education and state control be related to this basic problem of school finances? Compulsory education, assuming some system of enforcement was devised,[36] would have simply compounded the problem of overcrowding. State control appears even more irrelevant. The Provincial Government gave the M.C.S.C. around $15,000 a year and claimed it could not afford more. Would the creation of a Ministry of Education have transformed this situation?

The differences in the quality and quantity of public education in Montreal were a product of the unequal division of the school tax and this no doubt reflects the great political and economic power of the Anglo-Protestant minority. It is necessary, however, to go beyond this somewhat obvious statement and point out that an equal division of the school tax would have resulted in two impoverished school systems. The really interesting question is why the French Canadian elite exerted so little pressure to fund an adequate public school system when the Anglo-Protestant leaders were so active. It is difficult to resist the conclusion that the real problem for Catholic education was its sharp division along class lines. The Protestant Board was educating the children of the upper classes as well as the Protestant and Jewish working class. The quality of the Protestant public school system was therefore a matter of great concern to influential and articulate members of the City's Anglo-Protestant elite. The Catholic upper classes didn't send their children to the public schools and thus their interest in the quality of public education was limited. The failure of the Catholic community to develop a sustained campaign for a revision of the school tax split and its unwillingness to endorse increases in the Catholic mill rate stand in sharp contrast to the systematic pressure for increased funding from the leaders of the Protestant community.

Chapter 5

Housing Conditions

One of the most important consequences of low family incomes was the inability of most wage earners to afford the purchase of even the most modest home. Montreal was preeminently a city of tenants. Over 80 per cent of the population rented their dwellings and absentee landlords were the norm in Montreal. This may help to account for the poor condition of much of the housing. Certainly one of the most prominent features of the city in the first three decades of the twentieth century was the steady growth of "instant slums."

The description of working class housing which H. B. Ames had presented in 1897 emphasized the problems of poor sanitation, rear tenements, high density of population, and a lack of yards and open spaces. Overcrowding, the number of persons per room, did not "appear to be a cause for alarm" and there was an 8 per cent vacancy rate in the district. If Ames had taken a second survey a few years later he would have found that "overcrowding" had become an additional problem as increased immigration from Europe and rural Quebec placed enormous pressure on the already inadequate housing stock.

In 1904 *Le Canada* reported that there was a shortage of between 800 and 1000 dwellings in the city and this was a very conservative estimate.[1] Ten years later the Federal Government's Board of Inquiry into the Cost of Living noted that:

Housing conditions [in Montreal] have degenerated and there is a decided lack of workingman's dwellings with proper conveniences at low rental. Rents have increased by fifty per cent in the last seven years leading to a doubling up of families in the same apartment or house causing overcrowding and ill health.[2]

A more detailed picture of the consequences of rapid population growth was presented by one of a number of foreign experts who were brought to Montreal during the years immediately before

World War I when the housing crisis had become a public issue. The Secretary of the Philadelphia Housing Commission told the local Canadian Club of his tour of their city.

Only this morning I went round your city. Where I saw a house that had the earmarks of a slum, I stopped and went in. What did I find? Stairs that had been trodden by rich men and women; yet there were whole families living in single rooms – in some eight beds in a room; rooms without windows, rooms where the plumbing was defective and the floor covered with filth. Families with six or nine children occupied three rooms in the house built upon the rear lot – and you have many of them. I hesitate to say what I have seen here, lest I be thought to be discrediting your city. I went in one property here and found something I had never seen before: I saw toilets, old open toilets, seven of them in one narrow little court surrounded by houses occupied by ten families.... It follows from the character of these dwellings that you can have no real sanitary inspection here....

Do you know you can go down St. Georges Street and find almost every house has a cellar in which people are living, paying $10 or $12 for dark rooms? You must remember that children are born and develop there.[3]

The brief flurry of public interest in housing disappeared when the war began but the housing situation continued to deteriorate. In 1918 the pitifully inadequate staff of the Sanitary Inspection division of the Montreal Board of Health found that 1,868 of the dwellings they investigated were damp, overcrowded or dirty.[4] No valid statistical inference can be drawn from such a figure but the inspectors were overwhelmed by what they saw as a growing problem. Most of their energies were directed towards the review of requests for building permits and the city's Chief Sanitary Inspector complained that,

The inspection of dwelling construction has become more and more difficult in the past few years. The high cost of materials and labour are the main factors of this difficulty. The number of dwellings of low rent no longer meets the demand and attempts are being made to meet this scarcity by transforming existing houses built for one or two families into several smaller dwellings, but these do not always offer all the necessary guarantees from the sanitary point of view.... much discernment and circumspection must be used in the revision of building plans and specifications in order to assure all possible

71

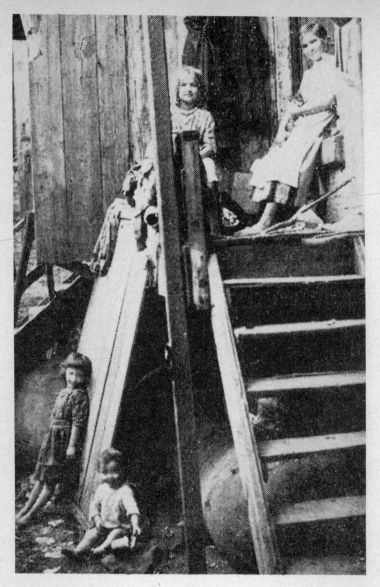

Slum conditions, 1912.

protection to public health without hindering the progress of construction.[5]

A large proportion of "new" working class housing had been created by subdividing older single family houses into flats. The middle class retreated to the suburbs on the edge of the mountain and once fashionable areas such as Dufferin Square[6] were transformed into teeming slums.

The construction of new housing on the fringes of the old city and in the adjacent working class suburbs seems to have been accomplished without regard to even minimal standards of decent accommodation. Elzéar Pelletier, the Secretary of the Provincial Board of Health, was a knowledgeable and determined critic of Montreal's housing practices. In 1908 he urged the city to enforce the bylaws of the Public Health Act which

> would prevent the construction of unhealthy dwellings which are being put up everywhere, for instance dwellings built upon land filled in with garbage, without covering the ground with concrete, dwellings whose foundations rest on damp soil, . . . partly lighted dwellings where rooms without a window are often seen.[7]

The following year Pelletier returned to the theme of new construction.

> As the city spreads the streets and lots are arranged to suit the speculator. . . . the city must plan with reserves for parks. . . . It must avoid the population density in the new wards such as exists in the old.[8]

The city continued to grow in response to the needs of speculators who insisted on making use of every square foot of the small lots. In some areas, such as Verdun, the flats were at least large, if badly constructed,[9] but in the east end cramped instant slums were built row upon row.

Ames had calculated that the average number of persons per occupied room in The City Below the Hill was between .86 and 1.09 in 1897. Arthur St. Pierre, in a post-war analysis of Montreal's housing supply, estimated that *for the city as a whole* the average had reached 1.4 persons per room in 1921.[10] St. Pierre's estimate must be treated with caution but there is little doubt that overcrowding had become a cause for alarm by 1921 and remained as a major problem throughout the 1920s.

The sanitary inspectors of the Montreal Board of Health devoted most of their energy to the correction of "nuisances,"

73

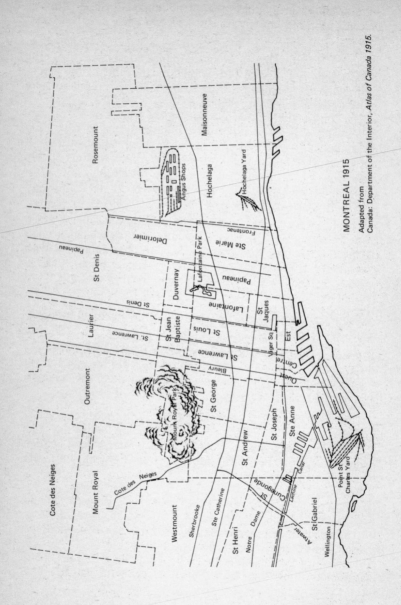

MONTREAL 1915

Adapted from
Canada: Department of the Interior, *Atlas of Canada 1915*.

such as dirty yards, the presence of dead rats, and plumbing defects. In 1901 the inspectors issued 12,863 verbal notices demanding the remedying of nuisances and 3,803 written orders. In that year they obtained forty-four judgements before Recorders Court for violations of the by-laws. No breakdown of the cases presented is available. Included in each annual report is a notation of the number of houses inspected which were "Damp" and a second group which were described as "Overcrowded or Dirty." Five hundred and eighty-seven dwellings were classified in these categories in 1901. By 1905 the inspectors were also noting the presence of "dark rooms," that is rooms without any direct means of ventilation. In that year 3,014 "dark rooms" as well as 223 damp dwellings and 261 overcrowded or dirty ones were noted as having come to the attention of the inspectors. Nineteen-eighteen was the record year for damp, overcrowded, and dirty housing, 1,868 dwellings being so listed. The number of such houses rises fairly steadily over the period though the number of "dark rooms" declines. It is of course impossible to draw any precise conclusion from such evidence.[11] Certain inferences may however be made. For example, it seems probable that the identification of housing problems by the inspectors seldom led to a permanent correction of the abuse. Many of the "condemned" dwellings must have been "condemned" every year. The extraordinarily small number of prosecutions per year suggest a similar conclusion. However, it is not really necessary to rely on inference in assessing the work of housing inspection in Montreal. The Provincial Board of Health and other observers of the city have left sufficient descriptive evidence.

The Provincial Health Board was created in 1886, and in 1901 its various regulations were consolidated into a comprehensive code, the Quebec Public Health Act.[12] The Act conferred broad regulatory powers on the Board but no specific set of regulations pertaining to housing were drawn up until 1906. Even after these regulations were established, Montreal failed to enforce them. Elzéar Pelletier commented on this situation in his Annual Report for 1908.

> ... not one of our municipalities has established an effective supervision over the construction of dwellings. ...
> Art. 40 of the Health Act allows municipalities to forbid the habitation of dwellings found unhealthy or overcrowded.[13]

The key phrase in the above quotation is "Article 40 ... allows municipalities." Under the terms of the Quebec Health Act, the Provincial Board could order a municipality to act in case of an emergency but it could not compel Montreal to adopt and enforce a housing code. Pelletier made four recommendations which cities should adopt in order to control building operations:

1. Give to the Municipal Architect power to reject plans that do not conform to Health Laws;
2. Appoint a Commission on Unsanitary Dwellings;
3. Create a "Sanitary Docket of Houses";
4. Obtain an effective expropriation law for causes of unhealthiness which, like the English Law of 1890, would base the indemnity to be granted to the owner of the property on the sanitary value and not on the revenue the owner receives.[14]

He also included a lengthy article entitled "Our Unsanitary Dwellings" as an appendix to the 1908 report. Drawing heavily on European municipal experience, the article included diagrams on orienting buildings in relation to the sun and the proper utilization of building lots to promote air circulation. With reference to Montreal, he wrote,

We shall not dwell upon plumbing, very imperfect in some cases, yet it is the part of sanitation which is better cared for. . . . we will limit our observations to lack of sunlight, lack of natural light, lack of air circulation, dampness and buildings erected on abandoned garbage dumps.[15]

Housing in Montreal violated good planning on all of these questions. Windowless rooms and dark "lightwells" were common and even the better class of houses being built in the city was based upon a floor plan which was "notoriously unhealthy." In addition, homes which had been built for the use of a single family were being "remodeled," creating "white mice cage architecture."[16] There was, Pelletier complained, no policy of loans to building societies and no involvement of life insurance companies in housing.

Pelletier's efforts to secure housing legislation met with little success. In 1911 the Montreal Board of Health proposed a municipal by-law "forbidding as far as possible" the building of houses with dark rooms and the "placarding" of existing rooms of this type.[17] Five years later, City Health officials reported that the by-law forbidding occupation of dark rooms was being evaded and suggested the passage of new by-laws which would forbid their construction.[18] This proposal was included in a report which summed up the state of housing regulation in Montreal in 1916:

...the question of the sanitation of dwellings has not up to now been treated with the attention it deserves. By-laws concerning construction regulate only the strength of buildings.[19]

The Municipal Board of Health recommended the preparation of a "sanitary house record" and the passage of by-laws regulating the amount of space to be left on each building lot, the abolition of small inner courts, and the regulation of distances between buildings.

The creation of a sanitary house record began in 1920 and was completed seven years later by which time much of the information was out of date. The Health Department reported that it had cards on 141,877 dwellings in 1927[20] but no analysis of the data was published and it is doubtful that any study was undertaken. The other proposed reforms were not enacted during the 1920s and the sanitary inspectors continued to argue the "urgent need for a modern building code." In 1924 the head of the Sanitary Inspection division wrote:

It is to be regretted that, in a large city like Montreal, builders owing to the high price of land show a tendency to use almost the whole surface for their building and to cramp the open spaces surrounding them until they become altogether insufficient for the admission of air and daylight into houses.[21]

The following year the chief inspector described some of the new construction in the city in more detail:

Flats are erected on lots only 12½ feet in width, they necessarily lack light and air because a certain number of rooms are built in a row.... Such buildings are usually erected on 25 foot lots upon which three to six tenements are built according to the number of floors.[22]

He urged the need for both municipal and provincial legislation noting that such houses were built in the "suburbs" as well as in the city proper.

The annual report of the Sanitary Inspection Division for 1929 contains an extensive review of housing practices in Montreal which provides a convenient overview of the housing situation in that year.

With the exception of a few districts in the City houses are built next to each other, upon lots of which the depth is about four times their width. These houses, as a general rule, are provided with exterior stairs which, almost in every case, obstruct the natural light in some room of the ground floor

New housing in the suburbs, around 1926.

and even of the first floor, as the stairs are used in many cases to serve for more than one floor.

In most of these dwellings there is a rear-room used as a bed-room, separated from the room lighted directly from the exterior, with curtains and sometimes with doors (in contravention to by-laws).

Two and three storey-sheds are to be seen in rear of these dwellings, connected with them with "gangways" which also obstruct day light.

The Sanitary Inspection Division recommended that so-called "double rooms," and any room that did not receive light directly, should in future be prohibited. The Division also had strong feelings about the size of rooms in the typical Montreal house, and about the squeezing of houses on tiny lots:

The present by-laws do not require minimal dimensions for living rooms, but it would be an advantage from the sanitary point of view, if such were prescribed; it would also be opportune to require a minimum width for a dwelling in order to suppress abuses existing since several years, which consist in building two dwellings on 25 feet.

With considerable restraint, the Division also observed that, "One should not lose sight of the inconveniences of cellar habitation."

Building by-laws limit the height of buildings and the number of floors, when such buildings are not constructed fire-proof. On the other hand, sanitary ordinances prohibit living in any basement or cellar of which half the height from the ceiling is below the level of the ground surrounding a building. But the case arises frequently when a builder is compelled to limit the height of the front so as not to infringe building by-laws and limits, from this very fact, the height of the basement above the level of the surrounding ground [is too low]. The permit and the plans are approved, the house is built and that basement floor is eventually occupied, unknown to the competent authorities, and in contravention of the health and building ordinances. This irregularity repeats itself from year to year; it would be opportune, in order to avoid too many interventions, that this sort of thing should be corrected.

Individual houses and the newer apartment buildings in Montreal presented no problem from the Division's point of view, but it did note that a strong tendency to cut homes up into multiple dwellings ought to be discouraged. The Division, despite Montreal's failure to improve housing conditions after a generation of discussion, still burned with the planner's reforming zeal:

> To solve the more advantageously possible, the housing problem, the future is to be entered upon with a general plan of rational development, multiply the parks, the playing grounds and the open spaces, establish "zoning laws" throughout the City's territory, change, as in certain European countries, the subdivision of lots favouring unsanitary dwellings; put into force a Building Code and a Housing Code which would permit to avoid errors of large cities of the world, such as Paris, London, New York, etc. where there are many slums with disastrous results as well from the economic point of view as from that of public health.[23]

In 1897 Ames had asked Montrealers to cease discussing the slums of Paris and London and turn their attention to the slums in their own midst. In fairness it should be noted that in the following thirty years some of the city's leaders did discuss housing conditions in their own city, but such discussions did not result in any more significant action than if they had continued to focus on London and Paris.

The housing situation in Montreal must be understood within the context of contemporary approaches to housing. The writings of Lawrence Vellier may fairly be taken as an example of advanced North American reform ideas on housing. Vellier had served as Secretary to the New York Charity Organization Society and had co-authored its 1903 report, *The Tenement House Problem*, which had led to the passage of "model" housing legislation in New York City. By 1910, when he published *Housing Reform*, under the auspices of the Russell Sage Foundation, Vellier was an internationally respected authority on housing.

Vellier was convinced that the "solution of the housing problem is to be found chiefly in legislation preventing the erection of objectionable buildings and securing the adequate maintenance of all buildings."[24] He was strongly opposed to the model tenement idea, pioneered in Montreal by Herbert Ames, on the grounds that it was a diversion of energy. "The experience of New York" he wrote, "where the greatest effort for housing reform has been made," showed that during a forty-year period "89 separate houses, providing accommodation for 3,588 families" had been built by "philanthropically inclined persons." For every

13 people housed in model tenements 1,000 others "have been condemned to live in unsanitary ones."[25]

Vellier was equally opposed to agitation for direct state involvement in housing construction. He accepted the apparent success of such housing in Europe but argued that "political conditions" were "totally different" in North America. "Who are the people" he asked, "who would administer public housing? . . . How are our city officers performing the functions with which they are now charged?"

> It would seem that we can wisely postpone so important an experiment until we have achieved better municipal administration of those functions of government which now engage the attention of the authorities.[26]

For Vellier the idea of state or municipal control of housing evoked a nightmare image, not of socialism, but of corruption and inefficiency and few observers of North American political practices felt inclined to argue. Public housing was seen with an equally unfavourable eye in Montreal. The platform of *Le Parti Ouvrier*[27] which may be fairly cited as the most "advanced" reformist programme of the day confined itself to demanding loans for workers to purchase homes.

One of the most systematic discussions of the various solutions to the housing situation in Montreal was published by *L'École Sociale Populaire* in 1912. The author, L'Abbé E.E.M. Gouin, P.S.S., was familiar with contemporary writing on housing in Europe and the United States. He recognized the importance of a major increase in the supply of low cost housing in the city but opposed direct participation by the state. Transferring functions to the state which could be accomplished by private organizations was to engage in a dangerous practice which would favour universal apathy and "réserver peut-être les advantages des logements officiels aux bons électeurs plutôt qu'aux vrais nécessiteux."

Abbé Gouin did allot a not insignificant role to the state.

> "L'État reste chargé d'un rôle considérable: stimuler les initiatives, les suppléer quand elles se montrent décidément inférieures à la tâche; cela peut aller loin, jusqu'à justifier dans certains cas l'achat par les municipalités de vastes terrains, la constitution de spacieuses réserves ainsi soustraites à la spéculation et destinées a se couvrir d'habitations ouvrières, l'imposition dans les villes en voie de développement d'un plan à suivre pour les extensions futures determinant d'avance et avec

précision l'emplacement et la largeur des rues, parcs et cours, parfois même la construction à l'aide des fonds publiques de maisons destinées à loger les familles nombreuses, car il y a là un problème que l'initiative privée ne peut absoluement résoudre."[28]

State action was not the primary solution and L'Abbé Gouin explored the other alternatives. He was much impressed with Herbert Ames' project and argued that other "capitalists" could earn more than 5 per cent on their investment by building in parts of the city where land was less costly. He also advocated the formation of building co-operatives by workers and the construction of houses by Caisses Populaires and other analogous institutions. But of greatest importance was the development of loan funds so that individual workers could become property owners and not tenants.

The Quebec Government introduced legislation "Pour aider à la construction de l'habitation dans les cités" in 1914. The Act was intended to provide a loan fund but it remained inoperative during the course of the war. Similar ideas had been discussed in Ontario and the Ontario Housing Accommodation Act, designed to encourage the improvement of housing, had been passed in 1913. The Toronto Housing Company was incorporated as a limited dividend (6 per cent) corporation to take advantage of the 85 per cent guarantee of bonds provided for in the legislation. The company constructed 242 cottage flats and 8 houses which were of excellent quality but no other enterprise was formed under the terms of the Act before 1921, perhaps because the Company was unable to pay a dividend until 1923.[29]

It was not until December of 1918 that the Federal Government entered the housing field. The Borden Government, using its powers under the War Measures Act, passed an order in council establishing a loan fund of $24,000,000 to aid the construction of low cost homes. The measure was part of the Union Government's post-war reconstruction programme and the funds were intended to be used principally to make loans to returned soldiers. The terms of the Act provided that any province could borrow sums at 5 per cent interest over a twenty to thirty year period. The provinces were to undertake the construction of homes or to advance the money, without increasing the interest, to municipalities which could in turn use it themselves or advance it to limited dividend construction companies. In the first four years of operation, the Federal Government loaned slightly more than $20,000,000 to the provinces, almost half of it to Ontario. Quebec was slower to take advantage of the scheme. New legislation, La Loi des Habitations Salubres, was introduced in 1919 and by 1923 the province had accepted 4.1 million dollars in Federal loans. The first report on the housing developed under the Act was not issued until 1924, by which time only 2,100 dwellings had been constructed in all of Quebec, 210 directly by municipalities, 1,190 by private companies, and 700 by individuals.[30]

For all practical purposes then the supply of housing in the City of Montreal was in the hands of the private contractor, as indeed it was in all other North American cities. Consequently the key to improving housing was the passage of legislation regulating housing. The chief problems with such legislation, according to Vellier, were the lack of clarity in housing codes and the granting of wide discretionary powers to housing inspectors. "The experience of most cities," he wrote, "shows that the granting of discretionary power has in nearly every case led to abuse and ultimately nullification of the law. . . . Pains should be taken . . . to state in the law precisely what owners and builders may do."[31]

The experience of Montreal, with regard to housing regulation, was similar to that of most cities. There was no clear, concise consolidated housing code. Wide discretionary powers were granted to inspectors and their appointment was determined by the politics of patronage. The Charter of the City of Montreal was substantially revised by the Quebec legislature in 1899. At that time housing standards were not specifically mentioned in the class of subjects within the sphere of jurisdiction of City Council. "Health and Sanitation" was the category that could be used. Under this general category By-law 63, concerning the regulation of "lodging, apartment, and tenement houses" empowered the City "to prevent the overcrowding of the same and to require the same to be put and kept in proper sanitary condition." By-law 112 gave the Board of Health the power to make and implement regulations "to promote the health of the city." Infractions of municipal by-laws were punishable by fines of not more than forty dollars and/or not more than two months imprisonment.[32] No significant amendments were made between 1899 and 1908 with regard to housing and the extensive changes of 1909, which involved the creation of a Board of Control, did not involve housing.[33] Nor were more specific enactments written into the by-laws in the remaining years of the period under study.[34]

Given the financial resources of the city and provincial governments, as well as the prevailing ideology on publically assisted housing (which was not markedly different in Montreal from other parts of North America) any significant intervention by the state in housing construction was simply not in the cards. But the development of a comprehensive building code was well within the ideological boundaries of the city's elite groups. Why then was so little accomplished?

Arthur St. Pierre, writing in 1924, offered this explanation:

D'abord notre population en général, et non pas seulement notre classe ouvrière, étant plus mal logée, la tâche d'assainir notre situation en est proportionnellement alourdie. La condition économique de nos travailleurs, moins avantageuse à certains égards, et l'âpreté de la spéculation immobilière apportent aussi leur part d'embarras. Mais ce ne sont pas là les éléments les plus troublants ni les plus caractéristiques de notre problème.

La tendance de nos compatriotes à s'entasser avec (cause ou effet?) l'extraordinaire prédilection pour les plain-pieds ou "flats" qui règne dans nos villes; l'étrange mentalité qui fait que l'on considère comme perdu chaque pouce de terrain que la construction ne recouvre pas; la mystérieuse hostilité que l'on a déjà soulignée chez nos gens à l'égard des arbres, et qui s'étend à la verdure sous toutes ses formes, si bien que là où des règlements de construction empêchent d'élever les maisons à la ligne du trottoir l'espace laissé forcément libre devient bientôt terre battue ou se couvre de ciment; en résumé: la tournure d'esprit, les habitudes de vie, les moeurs de toutes nos classes sociales en matière d'habitation, voilà l'obstacle formidable qui s'oppose chez nous à toute transformation radicale du logement populaire ou du logement tout court.[35]

St. Pierre's attempt to fall back on "les moeurs de toutes nos classes sociales" as an explanatory tool is regrettable. On other occasions he was able to offer a more fundamental critique of the prevailing social system. It is after all one thing to suggest that social attitudes (or climate) led to a preference for a type of housing which rejected the "norm" of a detached cottage with a private garden, and quite another problem to explain why such housing was of inferior quality. Pelletier had offered a plan for high density housing which avoided the problems of the typical Montreal block of flats and Ames had built a project which had much to recommend in it. A reasonable housing code properly enforced would have prevented the spread of the worst slum conditions. The basic problem and its solution were understood but neither the municipal nor the provincial government could be made to act.

Part of the reason for government inaction was undoubtedly due to the feature of contemporary reform ideology which Vellier most feared – the diversion of energy into grandiose schemes. No better example of such diversion of energy could be found in North America than the Montreal City Improvement League. The C.I.L. was founded in 1909 as a

> ... central clearing house and bureau of communication for existing city betterment societies ... so that by economizing energy, time, money, by federation, by surveying the whole field of municipal activities ... a central and solid unifying organization might be founded ... to make the strongest possible appeal when needed to the authorities and to public opinion.[36]

The C.I.L. was affiliated to the Union of Canadian Municipalities, the League of American Municipalities, and the American Civic Federation. It imported a galaxy of internationally known experts to address its members and developed a collection of books and reports on civic improvement. It advocated the construction of model tenements and "garden cities." It commissioned the Quebec Architects Association to develop a City Improvement Plan and set about lobbying the Provincial Government to pass a housing loan act and a bill to create a metropolitan planning board.[37] In short, the C.I.L. was the very model of a modern civic organization.

The C.I.L. devoted most of its energies to securing the passage of An Act to Establish the Metropolitan Parks Commission (1912) which created a commission theoretically possessed with sweeping powers. It could levy taxes, borrow money, expropriate property, and take other necessary actions "for the establishment of public parks, squares, promenades, boulevards, thoroughfares, recreation grounds, playgrounds, streets, baths and gardens." The Commission could also make recommendations "with regard to the improvement of working class dwellings." However, two things were required to bring the Act into operation: an appropriation of funds to get the Commission established and a municipal by-law empowering the Commission to act. Neither action was forthcoming.[38]

The C.I.L. and its Metropolitan Commission were viewed with considerable suspicion by many elements in Montreal. The City Improvement Plan, which was presumed to form the basic programme of the Commission, called for the construction of a series of new avenues and a number of parks, matters of slight priority to the majority of the population. The Provincial Government showed little interest in the Commission once it was established and with the economic difficulties of 1913-14 and the advent of war, the Commission collapsed. William Van Horne had become Chairman of the Commission in 1912 and his biographer provided this account of the Commission's demise.

> [Van Horne] set to work with W. D. Lighthall . . . and with him determined that the first recommendations should deal with the improvement of houses and the provision of open air spaces in the poorer districts of the city. . . . Olmstead was invited from Philadelphia to help them. But the Quebec Government had failed to make any appropriation for the Commission's expenses. . . . For four years the Commission sought fruitlessly to obtain funds . . . the furor for town planning died away . . . [Van Horne] suggested the Commission should defray, by personal contribution, the obligations they had incurred and then dissolve.[39]

The C.I.L. and the Metropolitan Parks Commission tried to operate without a popular base and without a realistic programme. The prospect of a 5 per cent increase in property tax to finance the projects of a Commission appointed by the Provincial Government had little appeal for municipal politicians.

The romanticism of Montreal's upper class reformers was further illustrated by the exhibition of model housing prepared for the Child Welfare Exhibit of 1912. Photographs of slum housing and a chart on Montreal's park areas compared to other cities were accompanied by injunctions to build model tenements and support a city plan. A model kitchen was featured along with a model living room "furnished in hand-made furniture" which "could be made by hand without too great expense by a man or boy with proper training."[40] Attention was drawn to Hampstead, a new "garden suburb" in which the infant mortality rate was only one-third of the city average. The relevance of Hampstead, an exclusive residential development, to the needs of the working class was less than clear. The City Improvement Plan was exhibited and it was suggested that "many ugly and unhealthy spots might be turned into beautiful places without additional cost."[41] It was noted that seeds were being distributed to children so that they could plant flowers in their back yards.

This "diversion of reform energies" is of course as limited and partial an answer to the question of why the city failed to act effectively in housing matters as St. Pierre's view that "les moeurs de toutes nos classes sociales" were responsible. The fundamental problem was that the municipal and provincial governments possessed neither the capacity nor the will to become involved in effective regulation of a free market economy. Since the issue of governmental impotence touches on the whole range of questions dealt with in this study, further exploration of this question will be reserved to the concluding chapter.

Chapter 6

Public Health

The connection between inadequate wages, poor housing conditions, and a mortality rate which marked Montreal as one of the unhealthiest cities in the western world was perfectly clear to many contemporary observers. Ames had established the very high correlation between poverty and premature death for the section of the city he studied in 1897. Mortality rates in the crowded working class wards remained at more than double the levels of higher income areas throughout the period under review. By the twentieth century medical science possessed the capacity to bring about significant reductions in mortality and morbidity rates without any change in the living conditions which created so much of the problem. But in Montreal gastro-enteritis, tuberculosis, diphtheria, typhoid, and even small-pox wreaked havoc in the lives of the working class long after such diseases had been brought under a degree of control in other North American and European cities. Why did Montreal have such a poor record in the field of public health? Some of the reasons are revealed by tracing the history of public health work in the city. The major statistical material on the comparative performance of Montreal with other cities as well as the evidence of the uneven distribution of the burden of high mortality rates within the city is given in Appendix "B."

Municipal public health services had existed in Montreal in an organized manner since 1876. The Health Bureau's designated functions were similar to those defined for local authorities under the British Public Health Act of 1875 and reflected the contemporary concentration on sanitary inspection.[1] The theoretical basis of such sanitary codes rested on the belief that disease was caused by miasmas produced from decaying animal and vegetable matter. Disease could be prevented, it was believed, if dampness was overcome, drainage and sewerage improved, and waste materials, "nuisances," removed efficiently. If a disease broke out a physical quarantine was imposed, to be lifted when the infected persons were "better." Shops, markets, abattoirs, dairies, and milk distributors were inspected to correct bad sanitary practices and condemn spoiled foodstuffs. The British Public Health system which evolved from these principles was something less than a complete success even within its limited concerns, because insufficient attention was paid to the appointment of competent, independent inspectors with the appropriate power to deal with violators. Still there is considerable evidence that the improvements in public health laws were an important factor in the decline of death rates in Britain. The general mortality graph for Montreal shows a steady decline in the death rate between 1877 and 1884, and one may speculate about the possible effects of the new health system, but many other factors could account for the changes.

The concentration on sanitary inspection which marked mid-Victorian public health in Montreal as elsewhere was challenged after 1880 by the series of discoveries in bacteriology which began with the work of Robert Koch. The practice of inoculation for smallpox had been understood for some time and much work on the "germ theory" of disease had been accomplished prior to the 1880s, but the burst of scientific creativity associated with the names of Pasteur, Cohn, and Koch led to a fundamental change in the medical approach to man's most deadly enemies. The isolation of specific disease-producing organisms and the development of therapeutic and prophylactic vaccines for the treatment of many of them must be regarded as a truly revolutionary change in the history of mankind.

The medical profession in Montreal was kept well abreast of these developments. The McGill Medical Faculty, even after the departure of Osler in 1884, was one of the better institutions in North America and the faculty of the Laval Medical School was equally conversant with the new discoveries and with their implications for public health. Unfortunately, none of this advanced knowledge was of much assistance to the victims of the smallpox epidemic of 1885-86 which claimed the lives of at least twenty-five hundred Montrealers, mainly the poor. The vaccination riots of that winter required the use of militia units returning from the Northwest Rebellion campaign to maintain order and act as sanitary police. The crisis did spur the authorities to action. The Quebec Public Health Act of 1886 was intended to serve the same function as Disraeli's 1875 legislation. Municipalities were required to establish health boards across the province and a provincial board charged with research and regulatory functions was established.[2]

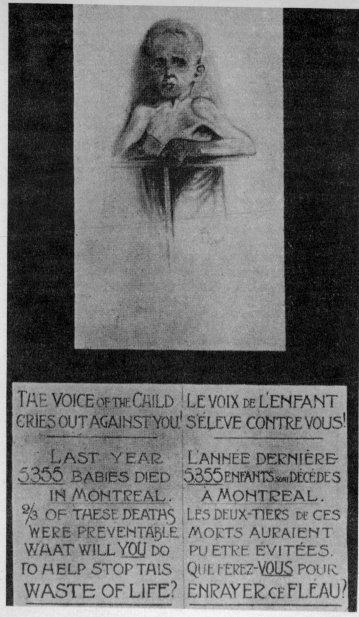

Poster for Child Welfare Exhibit, 1912.

The Quebec Public Health Act was unfortunately a very defective piece of legislation. The Provincial Board could force a municipality to create a local health board and the Act provided legal authority for a variety of public health measures, but no municipality could be compelled to enforce the regulations or finance an adequate programme. If the reforms which the Act made possible had been implemented in Montreal and vigourously enforced, then much would have been accomplished. As it was, even the question of smallpox vaccination was not adequately resolved for a generation. For one thing, after compulsory smallpox vaccination had been authorized in 1901, most municipal health boards failed to act.[3] As a result the disease could easily spread. It was not until the epidemic of 1903 that the Board ordered municipalities to undertake compulsory vaccination.[4] The Quebec Government's Royal Commission on Health and Social Welfare notes in its historical summary that only one death from smallpox occurred after 1918 in Montreal.[5] This did not mean the disease was eradicated and considering that more than thirty years had passed since the 1886 epidemic, there was little cause for self-congratulation in this belated achievement.

The inadequate response to the problem of smallpox was not an isolated case. The implications of the bacteriological revolution may have been thoroughly grasped by the Quebec medical profession but institutional responses were slow in coming. The Provincial Health Board did establish a bacteriological laboratory in 1894 and the Montreal Health Department included a second lab among its facilities but neither laboratory was adequately organized or staffed.[6]

In a speech before the British Medical Association, which held its convention in Montreal in 1897, the director of the Montreal Department, Dr. Louis Laberge, described the functions of the Department in terms of sanitary inspection of houses and streets, meat and milk inspection, and the disinfection of contaminated buildings. Laberge had a staff of twenty sanitary inspectors, four meat inspectors, two milk inspectors who were veterinary surgeons, and one disinfector.[7] The department was clearly operating in the tradition of the sanitary ideal.

Montreal was dependant for much of its public health assistance on the work of private voluntary agencies and specialized hospital departments. Ideally such private initiatives should have supplemented public facilities and pioneered new approaches to public health problems. It may be argued that this is precisely what happened in the long run, but such a statement would be too facile. It might be as accurate to suggest that such institutions quickly developed a stake in the public health business and instead of serving as pressure groups to encourage the adoption of vigorous, metropolitan-wide services, the tendency was to expand their individual spheres of activity without much regard for co-ordination or gaps in services. Large, heavily populated sections of the city were left without convenient access to public health services and the observer cannot help but be struck by the scarcity of medical and para-medical facilities in the heavily populated wards of the east end.[8]

The most important single force working for the establishment of a progressive public health system was the Quebec Board of Health. Its chairman, Dr. E. P. Lachapelle, and the permanent secretary, Dr. Elzéar Pelletier, had a clear understanding of what reforms were necessary and they conducted a vigorous campaign to accomplish their aims. The Board had to concern itself with public health throughout the province but a good deal of its energies were directed towards the city. Board members, and Pelletier in particular, were active participants in international public health congresses and organizations. Pelletier, for example, was made Treasurer of the American Public Health Association in 1897. The Annual Reports of the Board, as well as its monthly publication, *Bulletin Sanitaire*, contain a good deal of information about developments in Britain, France, and the United States.

The original text of the Public Health Act of 1886 was amended a number of times and major revisions were undertaken in 1901 and 1906.[9] The main reforms sought by the Board, apart from those dealing with factory conditions and housing standards which are considered elsewhere, were the enforcement of compulsory vaccination for smallpox, similar regulations for anti-diphtheric inoculation, the medical inspection of school children, adequate controls over the purity of milk and ultimately pasteurization, the development of treatment centres and sanitoria for tuberculosis, and water purification programmes. The Board did not merely talk about these reforms. Detailed plans were prepared and the by-laws of the Public Health Act amended to authorize municipal action in these areas.

The key word here is "authorize." The Board had limited powers to enforce some of its recommendations during emergencies but it could not compel municipalities to take preventive action. The reason for this is obvious enough. The provincial government was not prepared to finance capital or operating costs of public health programmes. Municipalities would have to raise the money for such expenditures from their own tax resources and public health, except in time of epidemics, proved to have a low priority.

Montreal's infant mortality rate was the city's most serious public health problem. Between 1897 and 1911, approximately one out of three babies died before reaching the age of twelve months. As late as 1926, the rate was still 14 per cent, a figure almost double the average for New York or Toronto. The single most important cause of infant mortality was "disease of the digestive system," usually classified as "diarrhoea and enteritis." Between 1906 and 1915 more than 42 per cent of the forty-five thousand children under two years of age that had died were the victims of "infantile diarrhoea."[10] By 1927 the percentage of such deaths had been reduced to 33 per cent of the total, but even this figure was substantially greater than in any other large North American city.

The importance of gastro-intestinal diseases in Montreal's infant mortality rate is reflected in the peculiar pattern of infant deaths in Montreal. Whereas in most cities the highest percentage of deaths occurred in the first month after birth, the crucial period for Montreal's children was from one to six months. Studies of infant mortality in other countries provide an essential framework for analysing this phenomenon. One of the standard text books on public health used in Canadian medical schools in the 1920s cited a study of infant mortality in England and Wales, where accurate statistics were available. In the conclusion of that work the author argued that:

> It appears then that under the term "infant mortality" we are classing together two radically different types of causes of death.... The first type consists of deaths due to developmental factors which vary but little from place to place, year to year, and class to class, and appear to be caused by fundamental influences which we do not fully understand, and at present seem unable to control. The second type consists of deaths mainly due to respiratory diseases and enteritis caused by influences in the post-natal environment, most prevalent in crowded, smoky, industrial and mining districts, and probably entirely preventable.[11]

Montreal's high infant mortality rate was due to "influences in the post-natal environment" and such deaths were "most prevalent in crowded, smoky, industrial . . . districts" of the city.

The Children's Bureau of the U.S. Department of Labour

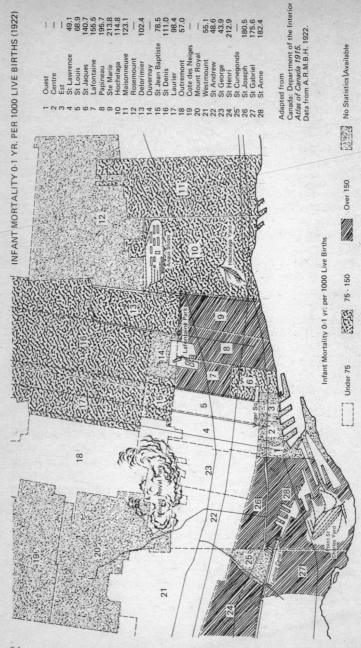

INFANT MORTALITY 0-1 YR. PER 1000 LIVE BIRTHS (1922)

1	Ouest	—
2	Centre	—
3	Est	—
4	St Lawrence	49.1
5	St Louis	68.9
6	St Jaques	140.7
7	Lafontaine	155.5
8	Papineau	195.7
9	Ste Marie	213.8
10	Hochelaga	114.8
11	Maisonneuve	123.1
12	Rosemount	—
13	Delorimier	102.4
14	Duvernay	—
15	St Jean Baptiste	78.5
16	St Denis	111.0
17	Laurier	98.4
18	Outremont	57.0
19	Cote des Neiges	—
20	Mount Royal	—
21	Westmount	55.1
22	St Andrew	48.6
23	St George	43.9
24	St Henri	212.9
25	St Cunegonde	—
26	St Joseph	180.5
27	St Gabriel	175.6
28	St Anne	182.4

Adapted from
Canada: Department of the Interior
Atlas of Canada 1915.
Data from A.R.M.B.H. 1922.

Infant Mortality 0-1 yr. per 1000 Live Births

Under 75   75 - 150   Over 150   No Statistics Available

expressed its views on the incidence of high infant mortality in a different way.[12] It defined a "Safety Zone" for babies which involved the following criteria:

a) The majority of fathers earn living wages;
b) Mothers are not employed during the year before or the year after birth;
c) Proper maternal care is provided during the period of child birth;
d) The father and mother are literate, i.e. able to read and write;
e) Proper housing conditions exist.

No comparable studies of infant mortality were undertaken in Montreal but the available evidence would seem to confirm the pattern described in the British and American studies. For example, in 1921 the infant mortality rate for the well-off suburban cities of Outremont and Westmount[13] and the upper income wards in west end Montreal was less than 6 per cent, while the adjacent west end working class wards had rates in excess of 20 per cent. Infant deaths in the older east end wards were also around the 20 per cent mark. The newer working-class wards in the north-east sections of the city reported considerably lower rates, between 9 and 12 per cent, but there is a high probability that this is the result of incomplete data. The city's unusually high infant mortality was clearly linked to the general problem of the condition of the working class.*

The Montreal Health Department never attempted to develop a statistical correlation between poverty and death rates but it regularly reported the data in terms of a simple ethnic breakdown. At first three and then four categories were used: French Canadian; other; Catholic; Protestant and Jewish. Consistently throughout the thirty years under review, the statistics showed a dramatically higher mortality rate among French Canadians, particularly in regard to infant mortality.

French Canadian doctors had long argued that the high infant mortality in Quebec was primarily due to the tendency of French

---

* The statistics on illegitimate children born in Montreal provide one of the most stunning illustrations of infant mortality patterns. Approximately three quarters of all recorded illegitimate children died before they were one year old. In 1924, for example, there were 1,114 illegitimate births recorded and 878 died. Of this number, 542 died between the ages of one and six months, suggesting what conditions were like in the crèches and infant "boarding houses" which looked after the majority of these children. ARMBH, 1924, pp. 21, 22.

Canadian mothers to wean their infants very quickly and bottle feed them, often on a mixture of beef extract and cereal – "la bouille traditionnelle." Dr. Sévérin Lachapelle had attacked this practice and argued the case for breast feeding in a series of books and lectures from 1880 onwards.[14] His theme was repeated time and time again in articles published in the *Bulletin Sanitaire* and the popular press.

Observers struck by the significantly lower infant mortality rate among the impoverished Jewish immigrant community in Montreal claimed "that Jewish mothers almost invariably feed their children at the breast."[15] It is difficult to establish the validity of this contention and since the statistical basis for the calculation of Jewish births and mortality was recognized as inadequate, no real basis for comparison exists. In fact, the problem of the validity of the city's "vital statistics" makes comparisons between ethnic groups very difficult. The highly organized French-Canadian parish network in the older wards of the city provided a well established mechanism for reporting births (baptism) and deaths. The same was true for at least the traditional Irish Catholic parishes. The Protestant and Jewish communities seem to have been far less systematic in registering and reporting vital statistics.

Nevertheless, it is probable that the French Canadian infant and general mortality rates were higher than those of other ethnic groups, for it is apparent that there was a disproportionate amount of poverty among French Canadians. The predominantly French Canadian east end of the city contained the highest proportion of low income wage earners, the highest percentage of female workers (including, it may be presumed, young mothers), and the least adequate public health facilities. It should also be noted that pasteurization of milk was begun in the city in the first years of the twentieth century, but prior to World War I only dairies in the English-speaking west end of the city were supplying pasteurized milk to their customers.[16]

The high mortality rate from gastro-intestinal diseases seemed to point to impure food and water as the direct causes. Montreal's water supply was adequately controlled by 1914 and this may help to account for the downward trend in infant mortality around that time. But the city's milk supply, which had long been singled out as the key factor in infant deaths, could not be as easily purified.

The provincial government had established a Milk Commission in 1900 and had drawn up a list of rules designed to regulate the conditions under which milk was produced. The Municipal Health Department also established sanitary rules for dairies and employed several milk inspectors to visit dairy farms shipping milk to the city. The inadequacy of even this limited sanitary inspection was fully revealed in 1914 when the Federal Department of Agriculture published the results of a bacteriological study of the milk supply of Montreal.

The investigators visited all of the major dairy farming districts supplying milk to Montreal and acquired samples of the milk at the point of production. In order to classify their samples, they had to create a "new" grade of milk, grade "D," which was described as "five times worse than grade "C" milk. The "C" category was used in North America for milk which was not fit for drinking but could be used in manufactured food. Twenty per cent of the 285 samples of milk sent to Montreal for ordinary consumption were classified as Grade "D" and 30 per cent were listed as "C." By the time the milk reached Montreal, shipped in milk cans loaded in ordinary freight cars, 90 per cent of it was unfit for human consumption by the standards used in large American cities.[17]

"Reputable" milk dealers attempted to overcome this by pasteurization but less than a quarter of the city's milk supply was pasteurized in 1914 and of the six large dairies investigated by the Commission, only one carried out completely effective pasteurization. The most common method of milk distribution was to measure a quart with the top of a milk can and pour it into a container brought by the customer. The big dairies bottled milk but the Commission pointed out that bottling was no guarantee of purity.[18]

This report recommended careful inspection of dairy farms, a strict classification of milk and compulsory pasteurization by controlled methods. The investigators also pointed out that New York City had cut its infant mortality rate in half by establishing pure milk depots in poorer sections of the city and suggested that Montreal should act along these lines.[19]

All of these recommendations and indeed the revelations about the city's milk supply had been publicized before. In addition to the constant warnings and recommendations put forward by health officials, popular newspapers like *Le Canada* had carried articles on New York's milk depots and the pioneering system of controls developed in Rochester.[20] A significant

La Goutte de Lait—Ste. Justine, 1912.

response had been slow in developing, but by 1911 three "Gouttes de Lait" providing free milk had been established in Laurier, Delormier, and St. Andrew's wards.[21]

In 1912 the Municipal Health Department began to implement the recommendations of a report prepared by Dr. Sévérin Lachapelle of the Laval Medical Faculty, Dr. A. D. Blackadder of McGill, and Dr. Elzéar Pelletier. As an interim measure, the report proposed the establishment of twelve additional "Gouttes de Lait" in the areas of highest infant mortality.[22] Six thousand dollars was appropriated to assist in creating the new milk depots and by 1914 the city was spending $17,420 on twenty-seven depots. In that year, 3,101 infants were registered with "Gouttes de Lait" and the Health Department noted that the death rate among those registered was only 50 per thousand, less than one quarter of the overall infant mortality rate.[23]

Lachapelle and Blackadder had recommended the development of a permanent organization involving the appointment of a number of public health nurses and the transformation of "Gouttes de Lait" into medical and educational public health centres. The war seems to have curbed the development of this more systematic attack on infant mortality. By 1916 the civic grant to existing milk stations was reduced to just $12,000 and there was a slight decline in the number of "Gouttes de Lait."[24] In 1918 the Municipal Health Department established an Infant Hygienic Division and the following year a number of municipal baby clinics, along the lines recommended in 1912, were opened. Civic action in this field had been slow in coming but by 1927 there were twenty-seven public and private baby clinics and 41 per cent of all newborn infants in the city were supervised by a clinic.[25]

The *Report* on Montreal's milk supply had suggested a number of regulatory measures. In 1914 the city's health officials had drafted a comprehensive milk by-law which provided for the grading of milk and the strict enforcement of sanitary rules. The by-law was not adopted until 1925, partly because of doubts about its legality, partly because of controversy about compulsory pasteurization, and partly because of City Council's inertia. However, in the intervening years, considerable public pressure had gradually built up in favour of pasteurization and by 1926, when the law requiring it began to be enforced, 94 per cent of the city's milk was being pasteurized.[26]

The perennial problem of the gap between legislation and strict enforcement was dramatically illustrated to the people of Montreal in 1927 when an epidemic of typhoid fever swept the city. The source of the typhoid virus, which killed 533 people, was traced to a dairy which superficially met sanitary standards and pasteurized its milk but the worker who turned out to be a typhoid carrier had not been examined.[27] Yet it must be noted that the campaign against infant mortality began to show significant results in the 1920s. An infant mortality rate in 1927 of 113 per thousand was nothing to be proud of and other cities had accomplished considerably more, but at least a basis for controlling infant mortality had finally been established.

The second most important public health problem in the city was tuberculosis. Between 1900 and 1918, the mortality rate from T.B. was always in excess of 200 deaths per one hundred thousand population, a figure which placed Montreal in a unique category among large North American cities. As in the case of infant mortality, the published statistics present some problems of interpretation. The mortality rate from T.B. was always much higher among French Canadians than among other ethnic groups. In 1927, for example, the Montreal Health Survey reported the following rates: French Canadians 167; British Canadians 95; Jews 32 (per one hundred thousand).[28] Again it must be pointed out that the system of reporting mortality was so deficient that some caution must be used in generalizing from these statistics. For example, descriptive evidence points to a very high rate of T.B. among the city's Jewish immigrant community and that is not reflected in the statistics.[29]

When the tuberculosis statistics are broken down by ward, a familiar pattern emerges. In 1921, St. Denis Ward with 202 deaths per one hundred thousand had the worst record and St. Anne's Ward was second with 186. Only one-third of the population of St. Anne's Ward was French Canadian but the vast majority were poor. The rates for upper income St. Andrew and St. George Wards were 50 per one hundred thousand.

Prior to 1909-10, when the Provincial Government appointed a Royal Commission on Tuberculosis, the campaign against the "white scourge" had been left entirely to private initiative. The Royal Edward Institute, modeled on Edinburgh's famous Victoria Dispensary, had been established in 1909 as a result of a gift from the Burland family.[30] The Royal Edward was as well equipped and as "progressive" as any T.B. clinic in the world but its services could reach only a fraction of the infected population. Even then the absence of adequate sanitorium facilities made it very difficult to "cure" cases which it was able to diagnose early enough for treatment.

The Royal Commission recommended the establishment of

additional clinics on the basis of one for every fifty thousand people, the building of a Preventorium, a Sanitorium, and a T.B. Hospital.[31] The Commissioners noted that the current practice was that every advanced T.B. patient had to be released from hospital once a satisfactory diagnosis had been made because no sanitarium space was available. Experience in other cities suggested that the T.B. morbidity rate was usually ten to twelve times the mortality rate. Applied to Montreal, this meant that eighty per cent of those afflicted with T.B., as many as eight to ten thousand persons, were not receiving any medical attention. (The commissioners used a Medical Referendum as a method of gathering information and the summary of answers is of such interest that it is reproduced in Appendix "B.")

For the next twelve years, provincial and municipal health officials and some citizens' groups pressed for the implementation of the Royal Commission's recommendations. Dr. S. Boucher, the city's Health Director, was particularly concerned with the construction of a T.B. hospital so that the most severe cases could at least be isolated. The Sisters of Providence were prepared to operate such a hospital but the City Council, while willing to rent a building to the Order, suggested that the $150,000 required to renovate and equip the building would have to be raised by public subscription.[32] It was not until 1924 that the Sisters of Providence were able to begin construction of the Sacré Coeur Hospital in suburban Montreal.[33]

The same year witnessed the formation of a new public health organization called "The Montreal Anti-Tuberculosis and General Health League." The League was chaired by Sir Arthur Currie and was composed largely of Montreal businessmen. Lord Atholstan, the publisher of *The Montreal Star*, was a prominent member and he launched the work of the League by donating $100,000 to the Royal Edward and Bruchési Institutes to open two new clinics, one in east end Hochelaga Ward and the other in St. Henri.[34]

The League rapidly became involved in a wider range of public health activities and in 1928 it financed a systematic survey of public health activities in Montreal. The *Report,* which is discussed in more detail below, described the city's tuberculosis services in the following terms:

The skeleton of a good service is locally present and some good work is being done along most of the essential lines. For a full measure of success, however, it is necessary that the activities of all agencies, public and private, be brought together and coordinated into a unified tuberculosis programme; that funds and personnel be made available to extend the nursing, medical, sanitorium, hospital and preventive services so well begun.[35]

Fifteen specific recommendations were listed in the report and it was noted that "many of these needs" had been pointed out by the Director of the Montreal Health Department in a report issued in 1914.

In 1910 the Royal Commission on Tuberculosis had noted that Montreal's mortality rate from T.B. was considerably higher than that of any other large North American city. Seventeen years later, the relative position of the city remained unchanged. The world-wide decline in T.B. death rates after 1918 (caused, it is believed, by the high death rate among T.B. victims during the flu epidemic of that year) was reflected in the city's statistics, but throughout the 1920s, Montreal's T.B. mortality rate was three times the figure for Toronto.

Between 1911 and 1921 Toronto had developed a "comprehensive plan" for dealing with tuberculosis, but as Dr. J. G. Fitzgerald noted in his review of anti-tuberculosis work in Canada,

...two or three provinces and some municipalities have lagged and their tuberculosis records indicate it. In those places where money, energy, initiative, and enthusiasm in the crusade have been expended, the results indicate definite reductions in mortality; where they have not, tuberculosis continues to take its necessary toll. Not because of social conditions, race, or any undue susceptibility to the disease but chiefly because of ignorance, and apathy, and an unwillingness to appropriate sufficient money to really cope with the menace of the great white plague. Public health in the special field of anti-tuberculosis work is purchasable as in all others and liberal appropriations will result in a reduction in the number of tuberculosis deaths.[36]

Tuberculosis continued "to take its unnecessary toll" in Montreal not only because of poverty and poor living conditions, but also because of the inadequacy of the public health system.

The city's poor record in combatting tuberculosis may be partially explained by the fact that "no specific remedy against the disease" had yet been discovered. A systematic attack on tuberculosis would have involved large expenditures on clinics, preventoriums, and sanitoriums and the required expenditure seems to have been beyond the capacity of the existing political system. But what explanation can be offered for the failure of the community to take the obvious step of organizing an effective programme for the control of diphtheria?

The history of diphtheria control reveals a remarkably consistent pattern for most of North America.[37] The discovery of the specific micro-organism responsible for the disease occurred in 1884. By the mid-1890s the use of diphtheria anti-toxin in the treatment of cases was widespread. Diphtheria death rates dropped dramatically from around 150 deaths per one hundred thousand population to approximately one quarter of that figure. Montreal's experience was similar to that of other North American cities until around 1910. For the next ten years the world diphtheria death rate continued to decline generally while Montreal's rate actually increased. The continued decline in diphtheria death rates in most North American cities was facilitated by the development of the Schick test which permitted the physician to determine if the individual possessed natural immunity to diphtheria, an important consideration when systematic attempts were made to examine large numbers of children.

The Health Department of the City of Montreal did not develop a systematic programme for controlling diphtheria in the period under review and it continued to present a major health hazard. By the early 1920s a new breakthrough in the treatment of the disease had occurred. A vaccine for active immunization had been developed to replace the antitoxin which conferred only temporary protection from diphtheria. Mass immunization of pre-school and school age children was now a high priority for most public health departments. It was not until 1926 that a major campaign for diphtheria immunization was launched in the city and then the agent was the Montreal Anti-Tuberculosis and General Health League, not the Health Department.[38] The death rate from diphtheria was as selective as other diseases. It had virtually disappeared from the "City Above the Hill" before the First World War but in the working class wards it continued to take a high toll of young lives. Much the same kinds of statements could be made about the history of other contagious diseases but such analysis would add little to the picture already presented.

The Provincial and Municipal Health Boards, some newspapers, and a number of private organizations had lobbied for improvements in public health facilities since the 1880s. Thus, there was no dearth of information nor lack of plans to cope with the crisis in public health. When the Montreal Anti-Tuberculosis and General Health League commissioned *A Survey of Public Health Activities* in 1927, the real purpose was not so much to gather information as to publicize well known facts. The Committee on Administrative Practice of the American Public Health Association was engaged in a consultative capacity and the technical committee, composed of local public health specialists, used the Appraisal Form for City Health Work prepared by the American Public Health Association. The appraisal system used was based on

standards arrived at as a result of very careful and complete studies of the public health activities in cities of a population of over 40,000. In each phase of public health service the standard has been set so that 25 per cent of the cities studied which were carrying on such a service would attain a perfect rating. It is, therefore, not an idealistic and unobtainable goal which is set but one which may be closely approached by any city which has a well planned and properly directed public health programme.[39]

The general conclusion of the survey was that, "Montreal's official and voluntary services measure only about two thirds of the best examples of such services in other cities of comparable size."[40] In fact, the results of the survey are even more damning when the details are examined. "Milk control" was graded at 57 per cent of the standard, "Communicable Disease Control" at 54 per cent (diphtheria immunization received one point out of a possible thirty), and "Tuberculosis Control" at 55 per cent. Other grave deficiencies noted included the general failure to provide prophylactic treatment of the eyes of new-born infants to prevent opthalmia, the cause of 25 per cent of all blindness.[41]

The *Survey* chastised the "municipal authorities" for having "been slow in accepting the modern public health programme as an official responsibility." The budget of Montreal's Health Department provided for a per capita expenditure of just thirty-nine cents as compared to an average expenditure in the twelve largest American cities of seventy-eight cents per capita. Even after the expenditures of voluntary public health agencies were counted, the estimate of sixty-nine cents per capita was lower than what all but two of the American cities surveyed were spending out of public funds alone. The *Survey* suggested that the city should allocate an additional $364,000 to the Health Department and recommended that this level of expenditure, which worked out to ninety-one cents per capita, should be reached within three years.[42]

The authors of the *Survey* had firm views on the nature of public and private responsibilities in the field of public health. "The care of the public health" they wrote,

is generally accepted throughout the civilized world as a state responsibility. Under modern living conditions, community action must be taken to protect the individuals who make up the community. In addition, certain phases of public health work required legal enactment and, therefore, an organized force to carry it out . . . .

The voluntary health agency is essentially a pioneer organization. Its main functions are to investigate new fields of work and having proven their value to create sufficient public interest to ensure continuation of the service.[43]

They had too much experience of public health work in Montreal to believe that the Municipal and Provincial governments would assume full responsibility. As a result, they recommended a compromise which would provide uniform standards and comprehensive planning while utilizing the existing network of voluntary health agencies. Private agencies would be financed by a system similar to that outlined in the Quebec Public Charities Act.

The Municipality and the Province would each contribute one-third of the cost of such work carried on by private organizations provided always that it is health work which is of proven value and that it is carried on according to a standard set by the public authority.[44]

Such payments would be made to private agencies only upon the recommendation of the Municipal Health Department.

The proposal to systematize public health work was not carried out and grants to private agencies continued to be discretionary. The budget of the Municipal Health Department did increase steadily between 1927 and 1930. Public expenditures reached a level of sixty-one cents per capita in 1930, rose to sixty-four cents in 1931, and remained at that level throughout the Depression.[45]

Chapter 7

Welfare

The casualties of Montreal's industrial system were many. Unemployment and underemployment were persistent problems; many workers, no matter how thrifty, found it impossible to make ends meet twelve months a year when they could find work for only eight. In some years, frequent recessions left a significant proportion of labourers unable to find any employment at all. The high death rate among workers created another class of the disadvantaged – widows and orphans. In a large, crowded city, the destitute forced their attention on the classes above them, if by contiguity alone.

The poor posed a problem of some delicacy. A society conditioned to laissez-faire principles found pauperism an abhorrent idea; the concept of making one's own way in the world was the very foundation stone of the social order. Yet, obstinately, the destitute insisted on being there. Fear of social disorder if the minimum needs of the poor were not met, as well as raw consciences, impelled the better classes to provide charity. But, in the laissez-faire context, it was necessarily stern charity, charity designed to be as uncomfortable and as demeaning as possible. Such a charitable system would meet the Christian duty of caring for real needs, while discouraging the vicious from seeking to make an easy life of pauperism. "Charity, not coddling" was the motto.

The city possessed an incredible array of charitable institutions organized along ethnic and religious lines. A *Directory of some Montreal Charities,* published in 1901, listed fifteen houses of refuge, thirteen outdoor relief agencies, fourteen old age homes, eleven orphanages, eighteen "moral and educational institutions," and more than a score of other miscellaneous charitable agencies.[1] These institutions had developed within the ideological framework of the Christian obligation to give alms and the tradition of welfare work carried out by the Roman Catholic Church since the foundation of New France.

The allegedly unique characteristics of Quebec's welfare system, with its delegation of power to religious and lay societies and the exclusion of the state from charitable activities, has been frequently noted. The issue of clerical control of welfare institutions has provided a topic for political and historical controversy for more than a hundred years, but very little has been written about the actual functioning of the various welfare institutions. The problem has been further obscured by the absence of a comparative framework and the tendency of non-Catholics (and more recently Catholics as well) to assume the superiority of "state" control. While it is not possible at this stage in the study of Canadian social history to provide a comprehensive picture of welfare institutions, it is possible to raise some questions and begin to provide some tentative and partial answers.

Two quite separate problems are dealt with in this chapter. In the first instance, the concern is with welfare institutions as they relate to the experience of their working class clientele. The available sources force us to look at that experience through the eyes of the charity workers, but no very large act of the imagination is required to relate the evidence to the lives of the recipients of charity. Second is the attempt to provide a partial comparative framework so that the situation in Montreal may be examined in a broader context and the unique features of French Canada's welfare system isolated. The comparison developed here is largely between the approaches of the Protestant and Catholic communities in Montreal. The implication that the policies and practices of the Montreal Protestant community were broadly similar to developments in other parts of North America is inferred from similarities in the rhetoric used – an admittedly dangerous basis for making such an inference.

The cornerstone of Montreal's welfare structure was the St. Vincent de Paul Society organized in every Catholic parish of the city. The parish committee, composed of laymen, met weekly to consider applications for relief and after investigation, it could provide food, fuel, clothing or cash to dependent families. Relief was accompanied by a certain amount of pious preaching but an attempt was made to preserve the privacy of the applicants. In 1897 the Montreal committees furnished relief to 1,500 families.[2] Between 1900 and 1914 assistance was granted to around 2,500 families per year, except in the winter of 1914-15 when 4,384 families or 20,686 individuals received relief from the conferences of the society.[3] Throughout the war years and the 1920s, between 3,000 and 4,000 families a year were the recipients of such relief.[4]

Protestants seeking direct assistance had to approach one of the dozen or more ethnic charity agencies, such as the St. George's Society; Jewish relief was organized on religious lines. In 1901 a professional social worker, who was brought to Montreal to work for the newly formed Charity Organization Society, delivered an address in Washington, D.C. to the National Conference of Charities and Corrections, in which he gave a description of "Organized Outdoor Relief" in Montreal.

... private charity, assuming in a way the position occupied by the country or city in a community in which there is public outdoor relief, has possessed itself of some of the worst characteristics of that form of relief – stereotyped methods and amounts of relief, officialism, and indiscrimination. For instance, the methods of a society I have in mind remind one very strikingly of the methods of boards of supervisors acting as poor overseers in some of our Western states. During the winter season almost any one of the right religion, and who does not appear before the board of the society in a drunken condition, is sure of getting relief, which invariably means a package of groceries each week, and a quarter ton of coal or a quarter cord of wood each three weeks, whether there be one or six in the family. I am aware that there are relief societies in other cities which have stereotyped methods in this respect also, but I doubt if they are anywhere as unvarying as in Montreal. And, certainly, relief societies elsewhere do not generally do such indiscriminate work, and do not force applicants to stand up before a board of eight or ten men and state their wants, and do not herd together 200 to 300 applicants in a room while their cases are being considered one by one; for the board I speak of only meets once a week, and no relief can be given out between the intervals of its meetings. There is no investigation except in very rare cases, and the questioning before the board is of a more or less perfunctory character. In other words, if I could suddenly drop one of my hearers to-day down into the meeting-room of this board while it was in session, without his having any knowledge of its character, I am sure that he would be convinced in his own mind that it was a public board dispensing public outdoor relief.

Of the four general relief societies having to do with Protestants, three compel applicants to appear personally before full boards at weekly meetings, and be questioned there.

Two only have anything which could by courtesy be called investigating. Three have practically stereotyped amounts of material relief.

Upon the Catholic side the world-wide traditions of the St. Vincent de Paul Society have effectually prevented its degenerating along the line of officialism even under the pressure of local conditions. The steady, sure methods of personal visitation before relief, of ability to order relief at any time, of secrecy so far as the applications are concerned, excepting at the conference meetings, are followed in Montreal, as elsewhere. But, if I have observed rightly, even with this society there has had to be a considerable stretching of its usual policy with regard to discrimination in relief.[5]

Francis Maclean, the author of this commentary, thought of himself as a modern professional reformer who was going to bring "enlightened" methods to Montreal. It should be understood that he, like most other experts on social questions of the time, thought that the proper role of the state was to maintain public institutions for the insane, the criminal and the "absolutely unfit." Private charity, relieved of the burden of worrying about rough shelter and sustinence for the total outcasts, was to concentrate on "right methods of relief." Such methods, he wrote, might include refusing material help and providing "the assistance of the alms of good advice" in the hope that "most of them will force their way to self-dependence under the necessary discipline." In Montreal, since there was no public almshouse, the assurance that the absolutely destitute would find shelter did not exist and the consequence according to Maclean was that

the poison of weakness and shuffling inefficiency and heartless sentimentality, which must always be guarded against in private outdoor relief, simply runs rife; and more than that, private charity finds its interests wholesomely centred around elemental material problems of bread and fuel.[6]

Maclean stayed in Montreal for only two years before leaving to accept the post of General Secretary of the Chicago Bureau of Charities, but his successors in the Montreal Charity Organization Society shared his views. The substance of their critique of welfare practices was that while the totally dependent requiring institutional care were looked after by state-subsidized clerical organizations, there was no poor house as a place of final resort; as a consequence private charity lacked "the spirit of sympathetic firmness which is often required in the giving or withholding of aid."[7]

Francis Maclean's complaint about the absence of a public

almshouse was partially remedied in 1912 when the City of Montreal received a bequest for the specific purpose of opening a municipal refuge. The civic authorities did their best to ensure that the Meurling Refuge was organized using the most modern guidelines applied to state indoor relief in the United States. Such relief, Josephine Shaw Lowell, the *grande dame* of American charity reformers, had written,

> should be surrounded by circumstances that shall not only repel everyone, not in extremity, from accepting it but which shall also ensure a distinct moral and physical improvement on the part of those forced to have recourse to it – that is discipline and education should be inseparably associated with any system of public relief.[8]

The Director of the Meurling Refuge provided this description of his institution to a conference of social workers in 1924. The reader may judge if it was sufficiently repelling to everyone not in extremity.

> To be admitted to the Meurling, one must be not intoxicated, must not have in his possession more than 25 cents, and must conform to all the regulations of the institution. The persons who desire to be harboured in the Refuge must present themselves at 5:30 p.m. and must answer all the questions put to them regarding their conditions, after which a search of the men's pockets is made, and everything that might damage the clothes while fumigation is being carried on is removed. Each man is then supplied with three checks, provided with strings bearing his identification number, and is taken to a room situated in the basement, where he is given a bag and clothes hanger. He must put his underclothes in this bag and close it, after having affixed to it one of the three checks given to him when his name was registered. On the clothes hanger he hangs his trousers, his vest, his coat and his overcoat and attaches a check to them; his shoes and his hat are deposited in a compartment bearing a number corresponding to that of his checks. The third check, which has a longer string than the others is placed around his neck. The object of this check system is to identify the individual when, on the following morning, his clothes are given back to him. The inmates' clothes with the exception of their shoes and hats, are placed in the fumigator, where they remain for thirty minutes in a temperature of 300 degrees.

Once the inmates have taken off their clothes, they go to the bathroom, where the soft antiseptic soap is put on their heads and, as the only known practical way of taking off the soap is with water, water has to be used, and that with rather beneficial effects. All the shower baths are put into operation simultaneously, under the direction of an official. After taking a bath, each man undergoes an examination in the physician's office. If, in the course of such examination, it be found that the person who seeks shelter at the Refuge, is ill, the superintendent must have him admitted to a hospital, in order that, regaining his health, he may again be in a position to earn a living and, also, in order to protect the other inmates in the event of the sick man being afflicted with any contagious disease. The medical examination has also another object, that of ascertaining the working capacity of those who seek shelter at the refuge, in order to find out the impostors who are in the habit of living at the expense of the community; this is a protection for the honest pauper.

Once his medical examination is completed, the man is given a nightgown, and he goes up to the refectory. A supper consisting of bread and a bowl of coffee or soup is provided. He is then taken up to the dormitory. He sleeps in an iron bed (the mattresses being entirely of metal) bearing his identification number. The bedding consists of two blankets, two sheets, one pillow and one pillow-case. The inmates must get up at five o'clock in summer and six o'clock in winter. All linen used during each night is thrown down the chutes, which lead to the laundry. The breakfast is served immediately after rising and it consists of bread and coffee.[9]

Between 1897 and 1929 Catholic charitable work in Montreal continued to be conducted along traditional lines. The St. Vincent de Paul Society used the same methods of providing direct assistance throughout the period and the major custodial institutions, orphanages, insane asylums, industrial schools, and reformatories, while subject to some changes in the nature of their individual operations, remained essentially committed to roles defined in the nineteenth century. When the provincial legislature enacted the Public Charities Act (Loi d'assistance publique) in 1921 it placed the financing of hospitals and charitable institutions on a firmer basis, but, as the Director of the Bureau of Public Charities stated, the role of the government was little changed.

With the exception of certain guarantees necessary to constitutional responsibility it (the government) contents itself with paying to the hospitals and charitable institutions a part of the cost of maintenance or of the cost of the treatment of the indigent whom they care for, while leaving to them the greatest possible autonomy and the widest liberty in the exercise of their good works. Our houses of charity, hospitals, almshouses and orphanages have long since proved their worth.... in no domain could their zeal, their devotion and their miraculous economy be surpassed. Justice and good sense exacted therefore that what I call the management of our charities should be left in such good hands.[10]

Just how good the various institutions were is a problem that only extensive research on a firmly established comparative basis could discover but no *a priori* assumption about the quality of these institutions seems justified. The following example of conditions in juvenile reformatories is intended to reinforce that idea and impress upon the reader the danger of assuming that the Roman Catholic Church was a monolithic organization. The different religious orders came to their work from different backgrounds and held different points of view.

Reformatories and industrial schools must be considered as welfare institutions directed towards the poor for it is clear that mainly working class children were committed to these "schools." In 1897 Montreal was served by four institutions which received government assistance. The Montreal Reformatory School was the chief institution responsible for the custody of "boys under 16 who had broken the law." The reformatory was operated by the Brothers of Charity, a Belgian order, which ran the school under contract with the provincial government. The director in 1897 was Brother Hilduard, a Belgian with wide experience in reformatory work. His successor, Brother Dominique, had been born in Quebec but had spent years in Europe as a reformatory director and as the organizer of a Catholic working man's refuge in Liverpool.[11]

Both men had very decided views on the development of a juvenile reformatory system and pressed their ideas upon the provincial government. One of the most popular notions about reformatories was the idea that they should be located in the country and the children taught to farm. The Montreal Reformatory, situated in the heart of the city, was frequently criticized on these grounds and Brother Hilduard offered an eloquent defence of his school.

I have no prejudice against farming but I do not think that the children of the reformatory school can be successfully turned into farmers. Nine-tenths of our pupils come from the towns and when they leave school will certainly return to their parents. What will they do with the agricultural knowledge they have acquired? Nothing. . . . We know by experience that what saves our children . . . is the trade they learn here. . . . The great majority of our children who remain in the reformatory long enough to learn a trade remain good; yes, at least 85 per cent become respectable citizens. Shall we obtain as encouraging results by teaching them farming?[12]

He went on to note the experience of Belgium where a large rural reformatory had been built but where few children were persuaded to remain in the country when released.

The directors of the school were able to persuade the provincial government to alter the practice of fixed sentences by allowing the school to develop a system of "time off for good behaviour." They were less successful in attacking the tendency of magistrates to sentence boys to common jails and in 1898 complained bitterly that seventy were incarcerated in Quebec prisons. During the 1890s there had been a sharp decline in the number of children sent to reform schools and in the years before World War I the numbers committed increased only slightly despite the enormous increase in population. The "sole reason" for this, Brother Hilduard believed, was the provincial law of 1892 which required municipalities to pay half the costs of board for delinquents. Delinquents were sent to jail or simply ignored to avoid incurring such costs.[13]

Prior to 1909 Protestant children from Montreal were sent to the Sherbrooke Reformatory, which was simply a wing of the Sherbrooke jail. In 1909 the Boys Farm and Training School was opened at Shawbridge in the Laurentian mountains and Protestant delinquents were thereafter sent there. The Shawbridge farm site was chosen "to isolate boys from evil associations" and to teach them the "science of farming and gardening as well as elementary education and trades."[14] There is a certain irony in the decision of the Anglo-Protestant community to embrace the land as a curative while French Canadian delinquents were prepared for life in the city.

Institutions for girls were much smaller and considerably less innovative. The Montreal Reformatory School for Girls provided elementary education, work in the laundry, and occasional sewing lessons. In 1905 the provincial inspector wrote:

We regret that a report has been spread that the nuns refuse to release girls to families because it is more lucrative to have them work free in the laundry.[15]

No further comment was offered and the validity of the charge remains unknown. The Directress of the Quebec City Girls Reformatory was also on the defensive against charges that girls were ill-prepared to obtain employment when they left the reformatory. In 1908 the provincial inspector. in replying to a request for funds to establish a kitchen to teach cooking at the Montreal Girls Reformatory, noted wryly that "the bill of fare of pupils and nuns is not such as would furnish practical instruction in the art." Women and girls could not escape the status of second class citizen, even in reformatories.[16]

The Montfort Agricultural Colony was the chief "Industrial School" utilized by the Montreal authorities for the care of dependent or neglected children. The Fathers of the Society of St. Mary had founded their "orphanage" at Montfort, a tiny village in Argenteuil county, "to remove children from the pernicious influence of the towns." The "immense majority" of the children at Montfort were under ten years of age and normally they remained there until they were fourteen. The provincial inspector noted that the exact age and status of the children were generally unknown because the children were sent to Montfort without records. The Fathers had acquired a large farm at Huberdeau, a nearby village, where the older children were given a chance "to acquire a taste for farming." Unfortunately, so the inspector noted, most returned to the city "in spite of efforts to induce them to become settlers."[17]

Quebec's approach to the care of delinquent and dependent children had much in common with the methods used in other parts of North America. The practice of contracting custodial care to religious orders or lay corporations was neither more nor less "progressive" than systems of state control. The quality of Quebec institutions seems to have varied widely but this was the case everywhere.

From 1900 onwards agitation for the application of "scientific methods" and the professionalization of social work developed rapidly throughout North America, including the Anglophone community of Montreal. The formation of a Charities Organization Society in Montreal was the first sign of this new direction in charity work. The Charity Organization movement had begun in London in 1869 and had rapidly spread to the larger American cities. The C.O.S. came to Montreal from the United States and its organizers drew directly on American examples in planning their work. The Society attempted to integrate the work of a number of agencies, including some French Canadian institutions, and its Board of Directors was drawn from socially prominent members of both linguistic communities. But the C.O.S. was operated in English and its efforts to be the "Office Central de la Charité de Montréal" had little practical consequences for French Canadian institutions.

The aims of the C.O.S. were spelled out in the First Annual Report published in 1901:

> The Charity Organization Society first and foremost represents the co-operative movement in charities – its aim is to form a common centre and means of intercommunication for all those interested in the welfare of the poor – not only for the exchanging of information, but also for the discussing of right methods and for the planning of those definite positive reforms which work towards the prevention of pauperism rather than its cure. For it is peculiarly the ideal of the charity organization movement to devote more attention to this higher kind of charity; the charity which is far and away above mere relief, the charity which means an uplifting of the whole tone of life.
>
> As more and more societies and individuals co-operate with this central society, and using the additional moral strength which comes through united knowledge and effort, more firmly insist that relief shall be given only when it does good and not harm, and that the welfare of souls and characters is of more concern than freedom from physical suffering, then more and more the possibilities for ultimately decreasing suffering and for making the lives of the poor richer and fairer will ultimately increase.[18]

The ideals and the prose were typical of C.O.S. rhetoric across North America. Francis Maclean, who wrote the above statement of purpose, provided a more specific account of the activities of the Montreal C.O.S. in his 1901 Report. He explained the function of the C.O.S. as a clearing house for information about poor families in the city and requested everyone "to co-operate in the movement for the repression of street and house begging." Ninety per cent of the city's beggars were said to be out and out frauds and the remaining 10 per cent required "care and thought and visitation" not "demoralizing alms." Citizens were requested to refer beggars to the Society. Individuals and organizations who were assisting poor families were urged to "make employment the basis of relief," to join one of the conferences of the Society and to "become a friendly visitor to one or two families; for after all the great aim of charity organization is not to decrease the amount of personal work in charity, but rather to increase it, and change its form."[19]

Conferences of the Society had been established in two parts of the city, Point St. Charles and the St. Henri-St. Cunegonde-Westmount area. The report quoted Josephine Shaw Lowell on the objects of the district committees.

In order to accomplish its object the district committee must point to higher paths and lead the way in charity. . . .

In all parts of all cities in these modern days there are plenty of people who are trying to do good to the poor, members of churches and societies of various kinds who are full of sympathy with suffering. . . . Unfortunately however they are often too ignorant to know that they are ignorant – they think that what appears on the surface is all that exists and it seems to them sheer folly and hard-heartedness for anyone to say that there is any harm or danger of harm in giving food to people who say they are hungry, in supplying money to women with wailing babies in their arms.[20]

The district conferences were to educate the well meaning to "listen to facts, and learn how to do the work they have undertaken."

"Friendly Visiting" was described as meaning "intimate and continuous knowledge of and sympathy with a poor family's joy, sorrows, opinion, feelings and entire outlook on life." An anecdote illustrative of the benefits of such visiting was included.

"One of the women we had not seen since she first came to us some four years before" writes Miss Frances Smith, "and we remember her distinctly as quite ordinary then. Imagine our surprise in finding that a certain dignity and earnestness akin to that of her visitor had crept into the woman's life."[21]

In addition to forming district conferences and encouraging friendly visiting the C.O.S. did co-ordinate some relief. Records of over 3,000 families were acquired and over 1,000 investigations were made. Outdoor relief was secured for 491 families, indoor relief for 89 persons and permanent employment secured for half of the 170 persons recommended by the Society. These activities were not financed by the C.O.S. which insisted that "no aid is given from the funds of the Society itself."

Francis Maclean's successor as General Secretary, Robert H. Lane, reiterated the purposes of the Society in 1903. "The new conception of charity," he wrote, "both preventive and constructive, has for its ideal the prevention of pauperism and the economic and right development of relief." In practice his major concerns were the abolition of street begging and opposition to "the custom of sending paupers and criminals, not only from the parishes of Quebec and of the several Provinces but also from the States, to be supported by our charities."[22] In 1904 he spoke out against the "great army of vagrants ... most of whom do not intend to do an honest day's work" and recommended a "farm colony ... where these people are kept under a firm hand and confined for quite a period of time." Lane also, while "not unmindful" of the growing evil of child labour, "very much doubted the wisdom at present of a special campaign" in this regard. He was greatly concerned about the "want of a thrifty spirit" among those who worked only during the summer months and recommended a campaign to restore "that spirit of thrift that existed among our forefathers."[23]

The next year the Annual Report summed up the achievements of the C.O.S. in the following terms:

> ... all human unfortunates crying for alms on our sidewalks have been placed in comfortable homes ... legalized begging has been absolutely abolished ... by the return of many destitute persons ... we have saved the city ... a vast deal of money ... we have taught the poor the wisdom of self-help and self-reliance, and the rich that by "disorganized sentiment" ... they rob the poor of those qualities which alone can lift them out of their poverty.[24]

The emphasis on investigation, organization, and moral uplift which marked the C.O.S. movement had been subject to severe criticism in the United States for a generation. C.O.S. workers did occasionally succeed in gathering facts about poverty but to many persons it seemed that the detailed investigation of "case workers" led to an emphasis on who was "worthy" of assistance rather than the planning of "positive reforms." Frederic C. Howe, whose book, *Confessions of a Reformer*, raised the hackles of many social workers, recalled how he had been led to question his role as Trustee of the Cleveland C.O.S. A local clergyman had written to him declaring,

Your society with its board of trustees made up of steel

magnates, coal operators, and employers is not really interested in charity. If it were, it would stop the twelve hour day; it would increase wages and put an end to the cruel killing and maiming of men. It is interested in getting its own wreckage out of sight. It isn't pleasant to see it begging on the streets.

I doubt, as I read my New Testament, whether the Twelve Disciples would have been able to qualify as worthy according to your system. And Christ himself might have been turned over by you to the police department as a "vagrant without visible means of support."[25]

Howe commented that he himself began to wonder if the Society was not "a business enterprise, designed to keep poverty out of sight and make life more comfortable for the rich."

The Board of the Montreal C.O.S. certainly fitted the Cleveland clergyman's description. R. B. Angus, George Drummond, L. J. Forget, J. D. Rolland, and William Van Horne, as well as a host of lesser businessmen, were directors. Whatever implication the personnel of the Board of Directors may have in an evaluation of the work of the C.O.S. it is clear that for the Society the root causes of poverty were individual rather than social in nature.

Robert H. Bremner argues that the Charity Organization movement in the United States "was a distinct advance in social thought: because it led to the recognition that poverty was an abnormal condition, that it was unnecessary, that it was curable and that its treatment required more fundamental changes than an increase in generosity on the part of the rich."[26] It is difficult to accept this judgment. In Montreal, at least, the "fundamental changes" called for by the C.O.S. were no different from the platitudes about poverty expressed throughout the nineteenth century. The Montreal C.O.S. did not endorse any of the legislation proposed by other reformers and in fact argued for caution on issues such as child labour, the abolition of rear tenements, and changes in the law on juvenile delinquency.

Allen F. Davis, a more recent student of urban progressivism, suggests that at least until 1905 "the philosophy of the charity organization movement led to philanthropy rather than reform."[27] Davis relates the gradual widening of the horizons of the C.O.S. to the influence of the social settlements and settlement leaders like Jane Addams. By 1905 cooperation between the C.O.S. and other urban reformers was symbolized by the election of Jane Addams to the presidency of the National

Conference of Charities and Corrections. If a change in direction was apparent in the United States[28] it was not reflected in Montreal and the local C.O.S. remained aloof from the struggle to reform the more obvious abuses of the industrial system.

The Montreal C.O.S. and the vast majority of the charitable institutions associated with it remained committed to philanthropy and largely indifferent to reform throughout the period surveyed. In 1912 the Society's list of "Constructive Reforms Needed" included the establishment of a separate court of family welfare, the coordination of hospital social service, the creation of a convalescent home and the development of adequate sanitorium facilities for T.B. patients[29] – all worthy causes, but far removed from the idea that the purpose of charity organization was related to the "planning of definite reforms."

It was not until 1919 that the C.O.S. showed signs of even recognizing the core of the problem. That year of high unemployment and social unrest led the Montreal society to title its Annual Report "Poverty: A Preventable Social Waste." Lady Drummond, President of the Society since the death of her husband, noted that upon returning to the city after four years in England she was more than ever struck "by the extraordinary beauty of the city . . . as one looks down on it from the Hill – and then on looking more closely the squalor and ugliness – the entire lack of symmetry and order in the city below the Hill." She went on to say:

> It is not for lack of "charity" that such squalor has grown and spread in our city. The number of charities is nothing short of amazing. . . . There is evidence that we are recognizing the causes of our failure, and that the energy and liberality of our citizens are finding expression in a new movement.[30]

The nature of the "new movement" was not specified and the tone of the report was defensive rather than innovative. But for the first time an emphasis upon social rather than individual problems was evident. A graphical analysis of cases investigated by the Society indicated that of the various "disabilities" unemployment and sickness accounted for 60 per cent of the total. A random sample of the homes of the Society's clients indicated that 22 per cent contained dark rooms, 15 per cent damp rooms, 32 per cent unsanitary plumbing, and 40 per cent no bathrooms. No specific action was recommended, however. With regard to unemployment, the Report declared that 20 per cent of the heads of families known to the Society were unemployed though employable. The General Secretary went on to ask: "What is it that throws their individual workers out of employment? . . . What is the relation between the wage scale and the applications to the charitable agency? Unfortunately we have not, as yet, gathered any information from our work which would enable us to give competent answers to these questions."[31]

The following year the Society undertook a further study of its clientele and reported that:

> The plain fact is that so far as the dependent poor are concerned, the sufferings of the poor themselves and the economic loss to the community are occasioned in great measure by conditions outside the control of the individual, conditions that only an intelligent and aroused public opinion can effect.[32]

It had taken the C.O.S. twenty years to recognize that "plain fact."

The attempt of the Charity Organization Society to apply "modern" methods of social work to outdoor relief was a retrograde step in the evolution of social assistance. Public attention was directed towards possible abuses in charitable work and the main emphasis of the Society was on rehabilitation of the individual guilty of the crime of poverty. This harsh judgement of the C.O.S. movement may be applied to almost all of its member agencies. In 1919 the newly formed Montreal Council of Social Agencies employed John Howard Toynbee Falk, an experienced social worker,[33] to undertake a survey of its eighty agencies. The Falk Report was a devastating critique of private welfare practices in the city. Falk began his report with a statement of the "fundamental principle" on which his work was based:

> Upon those who organize to alleviate poverty, cure the sick and reform the criminal devolves the definite responsibility of utilizing their experience to ascertain, reveal, and attempt to eliminate the social and economic conditions which bring their clients to their doors.[34]

In Montreal Falk wrote, Boards of Managers were selected on the basis of the "money attracting powers" of individuals and board membership was frequently seen as "a step up on the society ladder." Competition for financial support provoked jealousy and rivalry between agencies and in some cases the professional social workers were not permitted to sit in at board meetings because the worker was regarded as a social inferior. Social workers did not escape the lash of Falk's tongue. "I cannot help remarking" he wrote,

> that there is very little evidence to show that any large number have constantly in mind the fact that Jesus not only healed the sick and helped the poor, but also denounced the Scribes and Pharisees and forcibly drove the money changers from the House of God. In short, with a few exceptions the social workers of Montreal through lack of courage or failure to realize their full responsibility have neither as individuals nor in unison done much to prevent a recurrence of the social diseases with which they are in daily contact.[35]

The only organization which Falk singled out as a partial exception was the Montreal Council of Women which had provided "some means for concerted action, but even its efforts have been for the most part in developing curative rather than preventative work." Falk also attacked the agencies for failing to co-ordinate their work and keep accurate records, the minimal achievement that the C.O.S. might have been expected to accomplish.

One of the immediate results of the Falk Report was the organization of a united fund raising campaign for the Protestant charities. The Montreal Council of Social Agencies organized the united appeal and attempted to act as a spokesman for Protestant charitable work. One of the major policy concerns of the Council in the 1920s was a campaign to persuade the provincial government that the Public Charities Act discriminated against non-institutional care of dependent persons. In a resolution passed by its Executive Committee the Council developed a highly critical attack on the Provincial Government and French-Canadian charitable work.

> 3. That inasmuch as the policy of Protestant charity is to conserve the integrity of family life, the Family Welfare Association in lieu of the present grants made to it by the Province of $5,000 and by the City of $1,500 be given a per capita subsidy for each child under fourteen years of age of all families cared for by the Family Welfare Association and accepted by the municipal authorities as legitimately dependent families, such subsidy to be paid for by the Province and City through the Public Charities Act in just the same way as institutions now receive subsidy for children when they are admitted to the institutions. In this connection we would point to the extraordinary generosity of the Provincial Government

to the Sisters of the Grey Nuns in providing them with funds to erect institutions to accommodate several hundred dependent children, all of which are then cared for by subsidy from the Public Charities fund.

Must the non-Catholic minority be penalized because it follows the methods of caring for dependent children which now hold sway over the entire English speaking world and which have been accepted by the English speaking Roman Catholic authorities elsewhere in Canada and in the United States?[36]

It is difficult to decide whether this statement was more offensive for its arrogance or its inaccuracy. *One* Protestant agency had begun to place foster children and with the increased funds available from the federated appeal improvement had been made in other agencies, but essentially the member associations of the Council were the same bodies that Falk had described in 1919, following the same procedures. In fact grants were made to agencies involved in child placement and direct assistance, though the Council claimed the Protestant proportion of public charities money was less than their proportionate share of the population.[37]

When the Provincial Government appointed the Quebec Social Insurance Commission in 1930 the Commissioners asked Arthur St. Pierre, Professor of Applied Sociology at the University of Montreal, to conduct a study of existing practices in Quebec's welfare. St. Pierre replied directly to the critique of the Montreal Council of Social Agencies, pointing out that organizations like the St. Vincent de Paul Society, Assistance Maternelle, and the public health nurses "have gone to the homes of the sick and the poor . . . just as the protestant charity organizations have." He argued further that the available evidence did not prove that foster homes or "Cottage Orphanages" had been proven to be superior and referred to the high rate of turnover in foster homes. He added that Quebec orphanages had a very low proportion of true orphans and that families often preferred institutional placement because the institution, far from breaking up the family, "on the contrary preserves it by giving shelter for a time to one whom it helps and who will later return to his home."[38]

However confident St. Pierre was in his defence of traditional practices he did not fail to recognize the weaknesses which existed in Quebec's overall welfare system. By 1930 Quebec had fallen behind most other Candian provinces in four important areas.

Despite the early enthusiasm among some French Canadian leaders for a system of juvenile courts with probation officers the province had never gone beyond the reluctant creation of a single badly overworked juvenile court for Montreal.[39] The contrast in this area between the system for the protection of neglected and delinquent children which J. J. Kelso had pioneered in Ontario and the *ad hoc* arrangements for such children in Quebec was striking. A second area of concern to the Commission was the Quebec legislature's failure to follow the example of seven other Canadian provinces in passing a Mother's Allowance Act. The Quebec branch of the Trades and Labour Congress, the Catholic syndicates, the Fédération Nationale, the Montreal Council of Social Agencies and a variety of other groups had long pressed for the enactment of this legislation but despite the Commission's strong support a Mothers Assistance Act did not become law until 1937. The third major gap in Quebec legislation was in the field of old age pensions. The province did not pass legislation to permit its participation in the Federal Old Age Pensions Act of 1927 until 1936. Quebec's "backwardness" in these three areas was not the product of ideological differences about the role of the state nor was it caused by proccupations about conflicting jurisdictions – the primary constraint for Quebec as for New Brunswick was financial.

The fourth major weakness was said to be in the area of workmen's compensation and the history of the legislative response to the problem of industrial accidents deserves careful attention. The Industrial Establishments Act of 1893 contained a clause which required employers to notify the factory inspectors of accidents and the inspectors were required to undertake an investigation and to appear in court to offer testimony should litigation follow. The Civil Code required the victim of an industrial accident to prove that the accident was due to the employer's negligence. Winning such court cases was not easy as Louis Guyon testified in his 1897 factory inspection report:

> There have been fewer suits this year on account of accidents, and a great many cases won in the lower courts were reversed in the Supreme Court. In fact, decisions favourable to workmen are becoming rarer and rarer.[40]

Accidents, however, were becoming more and more common. Guyon described modern industry as "a real battlefield with its dead and wounded" and added that "each new invention, each increase in the rapidity of the means of production seems to carry in its wake a new train of dangers."[41] One incident described in the 1897 Report illustrated both the problem of new dangers and the prevailing concept of employee responsibility:

> On 22 November 1897 at St. Martin in the Convent of the Sisters of the Good Shepherd in their crochet mill, a little girl aged 14 years and five months was literally scalped. The child ... playful like all her age and imprudent also, jumped very high while near a shaft in motion; her hair was caught by the shaft and she herself, after being lifted up at each turn, fell at last to the floor all bleeding with her hair and scalp torn off. The poor child acknowledged that she alone was to blame for the accident.[42]

During the year 1899-1900, in one textile mill in Montreal, 23 accidents were reported, most of them involving the loss of a finger or hand.[43] Between 1890 and 1907, the factory inspectors investigated 4,608 accidents of which 263 were fatal.[44] This figure quoted by the Commission on Labour Accidents represented only those accidents reported to the inspectorate. Many employers simply did not make reports and among the recalcitrant employers were the Grand Trunk Railway and most of the firms employing longshoremen. Guyon testified that at least one in every three industrial accidents went unreported.[45]

Guyon's views on industrial accidents were strongly influenced by his attendance at two conferences held in Paris in 1900.[46] The sessions of the fifth International Convention on Accident and Social Insurance and the First International Convention for the Legal Protection of Work People provided Guyon with a detailed knowledge of European legislation. His immediate preoccupation on returning from Paris was the development of a "Safety Museum" which included photographs, models and actual examples of safety devices, including protective sleeves for moving shafts. Guyon hoped that the museum would influence employers directly but in addition he was able to argue before the courts with some success that the absence of a safety device constituted negligence on the part of an employer. The provincial government did not provide continuing funds for the museum and much to Guyon's regret it was closed in 1903.

The factory inspectors continued to press for a Workman's Compensation Act. Guyon attempted to obtain the active support of organized labour in this campaign but the unions showed slight interest. When a compensation law was finally adopted in 1909, Guyon remarked that the law was "entirely due to the initiative of the government."[47] Most of that initiative came from Guyon himself.

Public hearings on workmen's compensation were held in 1907 under the auspices of a specially appointed Commission on Labour Accidents. While some employers were flatly opposed to any legislation (one employer complained "legislators should promote instead of fetter industrial interests")[48] the important business groups supported the principle of compensation. The Montreal branch of the Canadian Manufacturers' Association and the Builder's Exchange went so far as to favour the adoption of the "professional risk" principle, whereby the victim's right to compensation would be assumed unless wilful negligence could be demonstrated. They were opposed to the existing trial by jury system because of the lack of limits on possible compensation and the cost of legal proceedings. Most of the spokesmen for organized labour supported the idea of compulsory insurance, based on a concept of professional risk as well, but the Commission accepted the argument of other business spokesmen who insisted that insurance based on the idea of professional risk would "place Quebec manufacturers on an unfair footing with other provinces."[49]

The Workman's Compensation Act of 1909 was the first such act to become law in North America. Pioneering had its penalties, however. The Quebec law did not create an independent board or make insurance compulsory. It simply established a procedure for claims and a schedule of payments for partial and total disabilities, as well as death benefits. If negligence or fault on the part of the employee could be proven, no compensation was payable. It was not until the early 1930s that the law was amended to create a modern compensation system based on an independent board and compulsory insurance payments. In the interval, seven Canadian provinces, beginning with Ontario in 1914, had passed acts which were well in advance of the Quebec law.[50]

The shortcomings of the 1909 legislation were a subject of continuous discussion after 1914. Organized labour constantly pressed for the adoption of the Ontario system and the extension of the act to cover occupational diseases which the courts had rigidly excluded. The Quebec Government eventually appointed a second commission to investigate workmen's compensation in 1922 but it did not begin its investigation for some time and it was not until 1925 that a report was finally issued.[51]

The Canadian Manufacturers' Association and other business

groups had actively opposed adoption of the Ontario system and they fought to maintain the *status quo* in Quebec.[52] They were temporarily successful for, when the act was modified in 1928, the Government failed to establish an independent board with judicial powers and allowed companies to purchase private insurance. Coverage was not extended to include occupational diseases. Indeed, apart from revisions in the scale of compensation and the extension of coverage from those earning $1,400 to $2,000, no significant changes were made.[53]

The resistance of Quebec's employers to a state controlled workmen's compensation system was typical of employer reaction throughout North America,[54] but in many provinces and states the battle for a comprehensive law was won before the First World War. The reluctance of the Quebec Government to act against the wishes of the major business groups on this question confirms the general view of the business orientation of the Gouin and Taschereau administrations. It would, however, be incorrect to exaggerate the importance of this point. The crucial question for the victims of industrial accidents was not whether the system was state controlled, but whether it paid adequate compensation. The answer seems to be that the Quebec system produced very similar schedules of payments to those in force in Ontario but only a full investigation of comparable cases in both provinces can provide a complete answer.

* * *

During the thirty year period under review, the City of Montreal grew from a small city of two hundred and fifty thousand people to a metropolis with a population of almost a million. It was probably inevitable that such rapid growth would intensify the social problems which had plagued the city in the nineteenth century. Catholic charitable institutions continued to operate on traditional lines providing whatever assistance their finances would allow. The Catholic elite was not isolated from contemporary notions of social reform but in the area of charitable work the Church had pre-empted the activist role. But the Church was not a monolithic institution and like the lay society around it, it was subject to varying influences. One group could be deeply involved in re-thinking the premises of its work while another religious order was tied to traditional approaches. Historians who wish to understand the role of the Roman Catholic Church in Quebec will have to cease using the notion of a "Church" as a convenient abstraction and examine the bewildering variety of persons and institutions of which it is composed.

The Anglo-Protestant community of Montreal had to rely on private enterprise in developing a welfare system. Its superior economic resources and the relatively greater emancipation of its wealthy womenfolk provided the society with a dynamism that was not always present in the French-Canadian lay community. The full current of English and American reform ideas was brought to bear on the anglophone upper classes and virtually no "progressive" welfare reform nostrum went untried in Montreal. The "organization" of charity work, the professionalization of social workers, the development of settlement houses, the creation of a school of social work, everything was tried except a direct assault upon the causes of poverty.

Many members of Montreal's upper classes, both French and English, were involved in what David Noble has called the identity crisis of the international middle class.[55] All of the accepted norms of society were being called into question by the growing complexity and disorder of the industrial system. Montreal was being transformed into a sprawling ugly anthill. Frequent strikes and the growth of labour unions seemed to foreshadow class warfare on a European scale. Against this impending chaos the middle class attempted to devise plans to re-organize society without altering any of the fundamental economic relationships. Such schemes were doomed to fail whether articulated in the language of secular progressivism or the phrases of papal encyclicals. The fundamental social problem was poverty, massive poverty, created by low wages and unemployment. For individuals, direct assistance limited hunger and prevented starvation, but the small section of the working class which regularly came into contact with organized charity was too often confronted with the "alms of friendly advice" and too seldom helped to achieve security.

Chapter 8

Labour Unrest and Industrial Conflict

The workers of Montreal were not passive in their response to an economic system which imposed such great burdens on their daily lives. Montreal was the scene of frequent and often violent manifestations of labour unrest. Strikes by both organized and unorganized workers constitute by far the largest number of *overt* demonstrations of unrest and we will, with Stuart Jameson, regard "strikes and supplementary tactics . . . as the exposed tip of the iceberg indicating a much larger but unknown magnitude of unrest that is hidden from view."[1]

The literature on industrial conflicts suggests that strikes are caused by a variety of factors which are an inherent part of the process of industrialization in a capitalist economy. It seems unnecessary to engage in such speculation about the causes of strikes in the period under review here. Strikers invariably sought to secure two main objectives: wage increases or, in the face of wage cuts, retention of the old rates; and job security. The latter objective was usually related to union recognition but unorganized workers frequently left work to protest dismissals of fellow employees. These two issues were of such overwhelming importance in the daily lives of workers that grievances like working conditions and the hours of work were of secondary importance. Organized labour's limited concern for projects such as workmen's compensation, minimum wage laws, and other legislative intervention must be understood in the context of starvation wages and the absence of job security.

In reviewing the pattern of strikes in Montreal over the first three decades of the twentieth century, it is impossible to avoid the conclusion that in situations where wages normally lagged behind prices, labour militancy was directly proportional to the rate of price increases. Workers could accommodate themselves to low wages by sending their children out to work or by taking in lodgers or by simply reconciling themselves to poor housing, a cheap monotonous diet, and other restraints. But when this accommodation with minimal wages was destroyed by inflation, workers were quick to respond by turning to labour unions and strike action. This is not to argue that there were no other factors which contributed to labour unrest. Stuart Jameson has summarized other "causes" of unrest in his book, *Times of Trouble,* but the importance of changes in the rate of increase in the cost of living seems to outweigh all other factors combined.

The information on the organization of union locals in Montreal available in the reports of the *Labour Gazette* and the *Quebec Statistical Yearbook* indicates an incredibly high mortality rate among unions but also points to a strong will to organize among the city's workers. The obstacles to union organization and meaningful collective bargaining were not peculiar to Montreal. Stuart Jameson sums up the problem in the following terms:

Labour in Canada and the United States has been especially difficult to organize for a number of reasons: high rates of immigration as well as mass migrations from rural areas to urban industrial centres, language and ethnic diversity of the labour force, the high mobility of the population, and the like. Employers, for the most part, presented an intense, and prolonged and at times violent opposition to unions. Up to the later 1930's, generally less than 15% of the non-agricultural paid labour in either country was unionized.[2]

All of the factors noted by Jameson applied in Montreal. The overwhelming majority of employers insisted on the "open shop," resisted use of the union label, and opposed the principle of collective bargaining. Of the 287 strikes listed for the city by the Department of Labour between 1901 and 1921,[3] 115 resulted in the total rejection of employee demands, frequently accompanied by dismissal of the strikers and the employment of scab labour. Success in the sense of employer acceptance of the demands of the strikers was obtained in only 49 strikes, most of them involving less than 100 workers in highly skilled craft unions. Some 70 strikes were identified as having ended in a compromise, but only detailed investigation of each one would reveal the meaning of that term to the employees. The existing data on strikes and lockouts in Montreal provided by the *Labour Gazette* does nevertheless provide considerable insight into the attitudes of the working class in the city.

The first two years for which *Labour Gazette* reports are available, 1901 and 1902, were relatively free from labour unrest. Eight strikes were reported in each year. A longshoremen's strike for wage increases and an increase in the size of work gangs was instantly successful, probably because it was timed as the last ships were desperately attempting to clear the Montreal harbour before the freezeup. The biggest strike involved six hundred cigar-makers who fought ten firms for wage increases and union recognition. The *Labour Gazette* noted that employers were using scab labour in May of 1902 and it ceased to report on the strike after June of that year. A small group of "boot and shoe lasters" seeking union recognition as well as wage benefits were also circumvented by the hiring of non-union labour.

In contrast, 1903 was one of the most conflict-ridden years in the history of Montreal. The *Labour Gazette* reported twenty-three strikes involving 7,318 workers. A strike of 1,200 street railway workers in February which affected 2,000 other employees was settled by wage concessions and a promise of consideration for their other demands including union recognition. In May, 1,500 employees staged a four day strike to protest the failure of the company to sign an agreement with the union. Mayor Cochrane prohibited parades and condemned the "outside agitators" who were behind the strike. L. J. Forget, the tramways company owner, replaced some strikers with "scabs" and announced that the strike was over. Conductors and motormen had obtained a 2½ cents per hour increase bringing their maximum weekly wage up to $11.40 for a 60 hour week, placing them well above the average wage in Montreal but still below the income required for an "ordinary family of five." Toronto Street Railway employees earned $12.58 for a 58½ hour week. The 60 hour week remained the rule for the workers in Montreal throughout the period. By 1911 weekly wages had risen to a maximum of $14.70, still below the "typical" level, but by 1921 maximum rates gave the conductors and motormen $28.80 a week, a sum very close to the necessary minimum budget requirement.

The second major strike of 1903 involved twenty-two hundred longshoremen who began a six week walkout at the end of March. The key issue was union recognition but the men went back to work with only the promise of "equal rights" for unionized and non-unionized labour. Fifteen hundred teamsters had come out in support of the longshoremen and in search of recognition of their own union but after twelve days they settled for a ten cent an hour increase. An electrical workers' strike ended after ten days when the two hundred strikers returned with neither a wage increase nor union recognition. A month-long strike of six hundred building labourers yielded partial concession of their demands for overtime pay.

There were nineteen strikes the following year and slightly over a thousand building trades craftsmen were successful in securing shorter hours and union recognition by some firms. The six categories of building trades craftsmen examined by the Department of Labour in its report on *Wages and Hours of Labour in Canada* were among the highest paid wage earners on an hourly basis. For example, bricklayers who earned thirty cents an hour in a sixty hour week in 1901 were earning fifty cents an hour in a fifty-four hour week by 1911 and one dollar an hour with a forty-four hour week in 1921. These high hourly wages do not of course reflect the annual earnings of such craftsmen.

Strikes in the tobacco industry were frequent. The cause of one such strike in 1905 was listed as "Objection to reduction in wages and employment of women and children." The results according to the Labour Department's correspondent were "Factory declared to be an open shop and company claims not to be affected." The most serious confrontation in this industry occurred in 1913 when over a hundred employees battled for eight months against a wage reduction. The company simply hired new workers and the strike died. A two-month strike of close to three hundred tobacco workers in 1916 won some wage concessions but strikes and lockouts continued to occur regularly.

Nineteen hundred and five was the year of the widespread strike of machinists in the Grand Trunk Railway system. The main battleground was Stratford, Ontario, but the issue, recognition of the International Association of Machinists, affected all parts of the G.T.R. Most of the machinists returned to work after the mediation of Mackenzie King had produced "an understanding" but no union recognition. Unionized machinists in Montreal were relatively well off. Work was more regular than in many other trades and their weekly income figures, $12.37 in 1901, $16.50 in 1911, and $39.00 in 1921, kept them above the poverty line provided steady work was available.

There were thirteen strikes reported in 1906, most of them involving small numbers of workers. The recession of 1907-08 at first brought "peace" to the labour front but in the spring of 1908 a ten per cent wage reduction in the mills of the Dominion Textile Company led to a strike involving all mill workers. The 1908 strike was the seventeenth work stoppage in Montreal textile mills since the turn of the century. Most of these disputes had revolved around wage questions and few of them had resulted in gains for workers. The 1908 strike was no exception. The workers were forced to accept a company promise that previous wage levels would be restored when trade conditions improved.[4]

The *Labour Gazette* reported a total of eighteen strikes in 1907 and 1908 and only four strikes involving less than 250 workers in 1909, but in the following two years a new wave of labour militancy developed and twenty-five strikes involving more than 10,000 workers were reported. Sixty-five "cloakmakers" struck for higher wages and were soon joined by 935 other garment workers whose ranks were only gradually thinned by employer resistance. There were still 225 garment workers on strike two months later but nothing was accomplished. During June of 1910, 3,700 masons and bricklayers struck fifty construction firms for union recognition and the closed shop. After four weeks the *Labour Gazette* noted "no settlement but nearly all workers return on employers' conditions." A second strike in the building trades involved 325 plumbers and 100 firms. The conflict dragged on for three months before work was resumed at the previous wage levels. The following year 800 carpenters went out demanding a five cent an hour increase. Most employers capitulated after a week but 150 were still on strike a month later. Strikes in the transportation industry, 150 warehousemen in June, and 200 freight handlers in August, led to the "replacement of the strikers."

The major strike of 1912 was the walkout of 4,500 garment workers who sought a reduction in hours and improved working conditions. After six weeks the strikers returned with an agreement to reduce the work week with wage increases sufficient to maintain the previous wage levels.

The impact of the depression of 1913-15 is clearly illustrated even in the brief summaries provided by the *Labour Gazette*. Only one of the fourteen strikes of 1915 resulted in victory for the workers, three hundred painters who secured a wage increase in April. The notation "strikers replaced" or "strikers returned to work at former rates" describes the fate of militant labour in 1913. The most serious strikes involved one thousand garment workers who were gradually beaten down over a six month period. Labour had learned a bitter lesson. Only five strikes were reported during 1914 and 1915 and unemployment was reported to have reached 25 per cent of the labour force.[5]

The war soon brought a return to a high level of productivity in Montreal's factories and intense activity in other sectors of the city's economy. Of the twenty-one strikes reported during the years 1916 and 1917, thirteen were described as "negotiations in favour of employees," two as "compromises," and two as under "arbitration." Close to nine thousand workers were involved in strikes during this two-year period. This pattern continued in 1918 though there were only six strikes unique to Montreal in that year.

One serious strike in December of 1918 involved the city's firemen and policemen who were seeking increased wages, union recognition, the dismissal of three senior officials, and the recognition of their association. Police constables, who were the most militant group, were receiving salaries of around $1,100 per year and demanding an increase of $500. The city's offer of $110 per year seemed outrageous, though the *Montreal Gazette* commented that such earnings would mean that policemen would earn more than skilled workers.[6] On December 13th, 1,560 civic employees went out. During the afternoon and night of December 13th, extensive looting of stores occurred and the city's "red light" district was said to be wide open. Violent incidents were reported at police and fire stations where "citizens" were attempting to provide minimal service. On the following day Lomer Gouin, the Premier, and Archbishop Bruchési intervened and after it was agreed that the three departmental heads would be dismissed and other issues arbitrated the civic employees went back to work.[7] The arbitration award raised the city's salary offer slightly but recommended against allowing civic employees to belong to organizations resembling unions.[8]

The strike had one other concrete result, the passage of the Municipal Strike and Lockout Act by the Quebec Legislature. This law, which was soon to be used against a similar strike by Quebec City police and firemen, enforced compulsory arbitration of all disputes involving municipal employees.[9]

The climate of labour relations during the last three years of the war was determined by the demands of the war economy. Few employers could afford to allow their operations to be interrupted and they were ready to buy peace with substantial wage increases. These gains were, however, wiped out by the rise in the cost of living. The "typical family" that could be fed, clothed, and sheltered for $14.15 in 1915 required $21.24 to obtain these basics in 1918 – a 50 per cent increase in the cost of living. In 1916 a Quebec Government labour official described this problem and suggested that

In the presence of such a state of affairs, the earnest and sincere patriots are quite right in appealing to the people to attach themselves more and more to the soil and to seek from it not only subsistence but also sound and real freedom.[10]

133

Such solutions were popular among intellectuals; workers turned to organization and direct action to secure a just return for their labour. Nineteen-nineteen witnessed a wave of agitation and confrontation such as the city had never before experienced. Sixty-two strikes involving more than thirty thousand workers occurred before the year was over. Felix Marois, the Commissioner of the Quebec Trade Disputes Act, attempted to explain the mood of labour in his annual report.

Neither revolution nor socialism is arousing the working classes today. No doubt there are ardent theorists and partisans of these dangerous doctrines in our province but the masses are ignorant of them. What the working class wants is improvement in their lot, fair remuneration for work and, above all, that living may not be unjustly made too dear for them. They admit that one who has a fortune may increase it but they will not admit that he should do so at the expense of the whole nation.

Against this they rebel and protest; they find that food and clothing cost too dear.... They were told that the country's greatest interests were at stake and they were asked to consent to such a sacrifice, the better to ensure the Allies success. But the war has ended and there is no change. Far from dropping, the cost of living is soaring to heights more and more inaccessible to the masses.

The people seek a remedy for the evil... but nothing is done. They become irritated, for they rightly or wrongly suspect the authorities of having allowed a band of profiteers to make large fortunes out of labour. The authorities have had enquiry after enquiry made but they only show more clearly the gravity of the evil. The masses understand nothing, they are driven mad for no remedy comes from anywhere.[11]

Perhaps "driven mad" is an exaggeration but the situation in Montreal in 1919 might well have given birth to madness. A strike at Dominion Textiles, involving thirty-two hundred workers, serves to illustrate the frustration of the working class. The demands were: recognition of the United Textile Workers of America as bargaining agent, a 50 per cent wage increase, a forty-four hour week, time and a half for overtime, abolition of fines for bad work, pay for time lost when it was not the fault of the worker (i.e., other departments slow), 20 per cent over day rates for night work and an increase in piece work rates. Marois tried to arbitrate the dispute but the company contented itself with the flat refusal of all demands and the statement that there was nothing to arbitrate. It regretted the "ill-advised strike" and declared "the mill doors are open." Two months after the strike began, the workers returned without having obtained a single concession from the company.[12]

Other large scale disputes in 1919 included a strike of an estimated four thousand carters who accepted mediation after fifteen days and were granted a partial increase. Three thousand ship-building employees were less successful, their six-week strike ending with neither a wage increase nor a reduction in the hours of work. A strike of two thousand wire workers ended after seventeen days when, according to the *Labour Gazette*, the strikers had been replaced.

The pattern of confrontation and defeat for labour continued through 1920 with ten thousand Montreal workers on strike during the year, but rising unemployment and the abrupt break in inflationary trends in the middle of 1920 cut into union membership and labour militancy.

The *Labour Gazette's* survey of strikes and lockouts for 1921 lists sixteen strikes for Montreal, only one of which led to an increase in wages. Three hundred iron workers and a similar number of boilermakers lost lengthy battles against wage reductions in the context of a labour market in which 50 per cent of metal trades employees were reported to be out of work.[13] In November of 1921, more than twelve hundred garment workers went out on strike in response to a call from organizers of the International Ladies Garment Workers Union. The key demand, "absolute and full recognition of the union," was strenuously resisted by most employers and a series of injunctions against picketing was obtained. The strike continued into 1922 but only a few shops reached agreement with the union. Before the end of the year, meatpacking employees, boot and shoe workers, and leather cutters had struck against wage reductions without success.

Conflict in the garment industry died down temporarily towards the end of 1922. Apart from the local effects of the strike in the printing trades which had begun in May of 1921 and was to continue until August 30, 1924, the only major strike of that year was conducted by longshoremen who lost a three-week battle against a wage reduction. There were very few reported strikes in 1923 but in January of the following year, the Amalgamated Clothing Workers launched a campaign to organize the clothing industry that was to continue for three years. Initially the union won a strike which resulted in an agreement providing for a forty-four hour week, the closed shop, and time and a half for overtime. This contract proved to be extremely difficult to enforce and throughout 1924 and 1925 the agreement was repeatedly violated. The A.C.W. held their international convention in Montreal in 1926 and the city was picked as a prime target for a concerted organizational drive. Between July of 1926 and April of 1927 a series of strikes, which at its peak involved five thousand workers, was conducted. Violence on the picket lines, arrests of strikers, and court injunctions against picketing were frequent occurrences. The A.C.W. was involved in a bitter internal battle with its left wing during the period and the Communist dominated Trade Union Educational League was particularly strong in Montreal.[14]

A general strike against all men's clothing factories was called for July 28, 1927. Firms which had previously recognized the A.C.W. quickly settled but two of the largest companies resisted vigorously. In September, an injunction against picketing was obtained and the union was sued for twenty-five thousand dollars damages. The union also attempted to confront the problem of employers moving their shops out of the city to avoid unionization and strikes were conducted in St. Jean and St. Hyacinthe. Union organizers were faced with hostile courts, a police ruling that all picketing was illegal, and growing employer resistance. They were also engaged in a bitter internal struggle with supporters of the Trade Union Education League which controlled two Montreal locals and was actively seeking control of the Montreal Joint Board. By the end of 1927, the Amalgamated organizers had regained control of their locals in Montreal but the drive to organize the clothing industry had lost considerable momentum. The A.C.W. convention of 1928 did pass a resolution authorizing the General Executive to launch "an immediate organizing campaign in Montreal, and nearby towns" but little in the way of new gains was achieved.[15]

Organized labour in Montreal, as in the rest of North America, was on the defensive throughout the 1920s. Union membership declined both absolutely and in terms of the percentage of the labour force which was successfully organized. The reasons for this apparent decline in labour unrest and militancy seem to be closely related to price stability.

* * *

One of the many untested assumptions made by Canadian historians is the view that Quebec workers were particularly badly served by the Catholic syndicates which began to be organized immediately after World War I. The notion that the Confédération des travailleurs catholiques du Canada (C.T.C.C.)

was a highly conservative organization which promoted "company" unions is based largely on unsupported allegations of persons involved with international unions who were quite naturally upset at the emergence of a rival organization. It must be understood that the C.T.C.C. did not come into the labour scene until after the militancy of other Canadian unions had been destroyed by the post-war crash and the vigorous counter-offensive against unions in Canada which was foreshadowed by the Report of the Royal Commission on Industrial Relations (1919). The policies of the C.T.C.C.'s executive must be compared with the policies of the Trades and Labour Council in the 1920s, not with a previous era of radicalism. Equally at the action level – the locals of individual unions – the comparison must be made not only in the same period but in similar industries.

The C.T.C.C. came into existence at a time when membership in trade unions was rapidly declining. The locals organized in Montreal were concentrated in industries which had not been successfully unionized by the international craft unions and in the prevailing atmosphere the movement achieved little and grew very slowly – but the same may be said for the international unions in the 1920s.

It is perhaps unnecessary to add that the pattern of labour unrest in Montreal was very similar to developments in other North American industrial centres. Strikes in Montreal were more frequent than in most other Canadian cities because a higher proportion of the labour force was employed in low wage industries such as textiles, boot and shoe manufacturing, and the needle trades, activities with very high levels of unrest wherever located. Jameson concludes that at least in the pre-war period, Quebec was second only to British Columbia as the major centre of industrial unrest. If this picture of relatively high levels of labour militancy is correct, the observer is left wondering why there was relatively little carryover into political action. Elsewhere in North America a strong relationship between unionization and labour-socialist politics appears to have existed. Why was this not the case in Montreal? Before dealing with that question, it is necessary to outline the history of labour involvement in politics in the city.

The political party that was to carry the banner of organized labour in Montreal was formed in 1904 with the strong support of the daily newspaper *La Presse*.[16] The constitution of the Parti Ouvrier de Montréal was copied from the British Independent Labour Party and the platform was a mixture of general measures common to most labour parties as well as items related specifically to Quebec. In 1906 the party nominated Alphonse Verville, who was serving a term as President of the T.L.C., as its candidate in a federal by-election in Maisonneuve. Verville was elected and was able to hold the seat through the 1911 election. He was a moderate, practically indistinguishable from a Laurier Liberal, but his election gave the party a certain prestige.

When the 1908 provincial election was called, two additional candidates were nominated. Albert St. Martin and Gustave Francq were men of a different stripe form Verville. Both were socialists with ties to the French left and both had a local reputation for radicalism. St. Martin flung himself into the battle for St. Jacques riding, which featured Henri Bourassa's successful attempt to defeat Lomer Gouin, and was crushed between the two "giants." Francq ràn slightly better in Hochelaga but still lost his deposit. The two men had attempted to establish a newspaper, L'Ouvrier, immediately prior to the election, but after only eight months it collapsed.

In 1910 the party was able to elect a moderate trade unionist, Joseph Ainey, to the Board of Control, but only after he had been endorsed by the upper class "good government" forces, the Citizen's Committee. Ainey was a "responsible" labour leader who subsequently joined the Quebec Department of Labour. Between 1910 and 1917 the party floundered, internally divided and unable to elect members to the federal or provincial legislatures. Two new labour newspapers, Le Progrès Ouvrier and Le Monde Ouvrier, were established but it was not until the national Trades and Labour Council sent out the call for political action in 1917 that a temporary revitalization of the party occurred. The party, reorganized as the Quebec branch of the Independent Labour Party, ran a candidate in Maisonneuve in the 1917 election but the anti-conscription vote was not to be diverted from the Laurier Liberals. The following year Joseph Ainey contested the mayoralty election but his opponent, Médéric Martin, won easily. It was in the provincial election of 1919 that the party won its greatest success, electing two members to the legislature. The 1923 provincial election was the last stand for the Parti Ouvrier. All five of its candidates were defeated and no further attempts at political action were undertaken in the twenties.

All in all this is an unimpressive record but then no laboursocialist party enjoyed much more success in Canada except in the years 1917-21. Labour's political strength in those years was closely related to opposition to the policies of the Conservative and Unionist Governments. Registration, conscription, war profiteering, government by Order in Council under the War Measures Act – these were the issues which gave labour candidates in Ontario, Manitoba, and British Columbia an opportunity to broaden their support. In Quebec the Liberals had placed themselves squarely in opposition to precisely these issues and the wonder is that any form of labour political activity was possible in the province. The decline in both political and trade union activity in the 1920s parallels the pattern in other parts of Canada. The war and immediate post-war experience helped to polarize some Canadian communities, but it served only as a means of reinforcing an artificial national unity in French Canada.

Chapter 9

Conclusion

On the basis of the evidence given in the preceding chapters, it seems necessary to conclude that the conditions of life for the working class population of Montreal improved only very slightly between 1897 and 1929. The major changes were in the field of public health, where the city's record, though still poor in comparison with other large urban centres, represented an enormous improvement over conditions at the turn of the century. But the creation of a safe water supply, the pasteurization of milk, and other measures which offered partial control of disease were not directed specifically at the working class. Indeed it may be argued that progress was possible precisely because health problems affected the entire society not just the working class.

On issues which were of direct concern only to the working class progress was slight indeed. In matters like housing, parks and playgrounds, welfare institutions, and schools, only token improvements can be noted. The slight reduction in the length of the work week may well have been offset by the greater distances that workers had to travel as the city spread out over the island. The most fundamental issue for the working class – subsistence wages – remained unresolved throughout the three decades. Family incomes may have been temporarily higher in the late 1920s than at any previous time, but the winter of 1929-30 proved just how short-lived this modest achievement was to be.

The problem of inadequate incomes for a life of "health and decency" existed for the vast majority of the industrial working class throughout North America but the evidence suggests that the problem was particularly acute in Montreal, at least in comparison to Toronto, the city which both tradition and logic indicate should be used for comparative purposes. Despite a shorter work week, average incomes in comparable occupations in Toronto were slightly higher than they were in Montreal. Hourly rates, while slightly lower in Montreal, do not account for the differences, particularly in view of the longer hours worked in Montreal. The most important variable is the much higher level of seasonal unemployment in Montreal. Leonard Marsh studied this question in detail using the new material made available by the Dominion Bureau of Statistics after 1926. Marsh concluded:

> The net range of seasonal fluctuation in Montreal (10 to 11 per cent) is not much greater than that for Canadian industry as a whole. It is greater, however, than that in any of the other major cities of the Dominion. The net range is lowest (about 5 per cent) in Toronto.... [1]

Canada, he concluded, is an "eight-months country" and Montreal an eight-months city. This pattern was particularly pronounced in building construction and transportation where the effects of Montreal's much more severe winter and heavier snowfall are immediately apparent.

The dimensions of poverty were greater in Montreal for other reasons as well. One of the most striking features of the occupational profiles of the two cities is the high proportion of unskilled labourers in Montreal, constituting more than one-sixth of the labour force as compared to less than one-tenth for Toronto. Professional occupations, by way of contrast, accounted for 4.7 per cent of the gainfully employed in Montreal and 7.6 per cent in Toronto. The proportion of skilled and responsible workers in the two cities show similar divergences in favour of Toronto. [2]

A simple explanation for these differences can be found by examining the types of industry then located in the two cities. Not surprisingly, Toronto turns out to have had a much higher proportion of employment opportunities for skilled, semi-skilled, and responsible workers. One of the best illustrations of this situation was the iron and steel industry which, in Toronto, was heavily weighted towards the production of machinery, agricultural implements, land vehicles, and the products of machine shops, while in Montreal industrial products of the hardware variety predominated. In the textile category, Montreal's production was concentrated in primary materials, thread, yarn, and cloth, whereas Toronto's equivalent activity was "hosiery and knit goods," not a high wage industry except in comparison to cotton textiles. Other important structural differences may be briefly noted. Printing and publishing, a high wage industry with a high degree of unionization, employed 15 per cent of the manufacturing labour force in Toronto compared to just 7 per

141

Notre Dame Street and 1st Avenue Viau, 1907.

cent in Montreal. Tobacco and leather products, notoriously low wage industries, accounted for 14 per cent of all manufacturing jobs in Montreal, while the figure for Toronto was 4 per cent.[3]

What accounts for the differences in the structure of the two urban economies? Since the dominant entrepreneurial group in Montreal was as anglophone and Protestant as it was in Toronto, the old Protestant ethic argument had best be put back on the shelf.[4] Equally dubious in view of the enormous horizontal mobility of labour are arguments based on the view that the French-Canadian workers, straight off the farm, lacked the skills to compete in a sophisticated industrial economy. They may have been unskilled but they came to Montreal *because* there were jobs for such workers. Skilled workers from Europe were attracted to Montreal to fill jobs on the railways, in Vickers Shipyards, and in other enterprises and if there were more opportunities for skilled workers, there would have been immigrants to fill them. The grading of a work force is primarily a function of the kind of industrial opportunity in an area and the Montreal region provided fewer opportunities for skilled workers than Toronto.

If labour was mobile and capital equally free to move, the basis for the structural differences must lie in differences in locational factors. For workers, the great flaw in the Montreal economy was the importance of a harbour which was effectively closed for four months a year. The shipping companies, the wholesale trading establishments, the warehouses, the railroads, and an unknown number of other industries were locked into an eight month season which, while no doubt profitable for the owners of capital, was disastrous for wage earners. The Toronto harbour was far less important in terms of both direct and indirect employment.[5]

Toronto, like the rest of urban southern Ontario, possessed a number of other economic advantages, the most important of which was the relative prosperity of the agricultural economy in comparison to Quebec. Ontario farms were more capital intensive and provided a far richer market for the products of small and large manufacturers. Firms like the McLaughlin Carriage Works and the Massey agricultural implements company were in their first stages dependent on a strong local demand for their products. Their later growth was only possible because of that initial strength. Quebec agriculture was labour intensive, unmechanized, and consequently far less likely to complement a local manufacturing sector.

In sum, the basic point made by Faucher and Lamontagne

that "Quebec industrialization had nothing specific to do with, and was not fundamentally influenced by its cultural environment; that rather, it was a mere regional manifestation of the overall economic evolution of the North American continent,"[6] needs only to be modified by paying greater attention to specific geographical differences between the Quebec region and other parts of North America.

Other factors which contributed to the much greater amount of poverty in Montreal may be briefly noted. The average family in Montreal was larger than in Toronto, 4.45 persons versus 3.75.[7] The average number of persons per family wholly supported by the head of the family was similarly higher, 4.0 in Montreal as against 3.41 in Toronto.[8] When these figures are related to incomes and expressed as the "Average Earnings of the Head of the Family According to the Number of Persons per Family Supported," the size of the income gap between the two cities is dramatically illustrated. In 1921 a family head in Toronto had available $426.00 per person supported as against only $313.00 per person in Montreal.[9]

The age composition of a family has a considerable effect on the labour force participation rate and essentially we are simply looking at the other side of the coin when noting that there was a higher level of employment per thousand of population in Toronto than in Montreal. The average number of children per family under 15 in Montreal was 1.75, while it was just 1.22 in Toronto.[10]

The evidence presented in this study suggests that the working class in Montreal was also disadvantaged with regard to the level of public services and the quality of regulatory legislation. This is most evident in the areas of public health and housing. In each of these areas the state was less effective than it was in Toronto and many other North American cities. This problem must, in the first instance, be tied to the relatively greater degree of poverty in Montreal, that is, the dimensions of the problems were greater in Montreal than in Toronto because of more widespread poverty. However, the response to the crisis in social conditions in Montreal was so much less adequate that a more detailed analysis of the role of the municipal and provincial governments is required.

The crucial variable was public finance, not ideology. There were few differences between Quebec and the rest of North America with regard to the kind of social reforms which were advocated. The Montreal Health Department and the key officials in Quebec City recommended legislation which was broadly similar to that passed in "progressive" civic and provincial administrations throughout North America and there was broad consensus on the need for such legislative reform. Indeed if one limits the enquiry to the kind of legislation passed by the provincial government without checking to see how it was enforced or if it was enforced, the record of the Gouin and Taschereau administrations parallels the record of most other provincial and state governments. It may be that studies of the actual workings of social legislation in Ontario would show a similar failure to enforce what was on the statute books, but the much larger per capita expenditure on health and welfare activities in Ontario suggests that there were important differences.

Per Capita Expenditures in Dollars 1926 – Ontario and Quebec Provincial Governments[11]

	Debt Charges	Legislation & Justice	Education & Social Institutions	Public Works & Highways	Agric.	Lands, Forests, Colonization	Other
Quebec	1.60	1.00	1.00	2.00	.57	.96	1.6
Ontario	2.91	.67	5.29	1.08	.61	1.17	.52
Total							
Quebec	9.3						
Ontario	12.29						

Per Capita Revenue in Dollars 1926 – Ontario and Quebec Provincial Governments[12]

	Federal Subsidy	Auto-mobiles	Corporation Tax	Succession Duties	Liquor	Lands & Forests	Misc.	TOTAL
Quebec	.82	1.35	.89	.82	1.25	2.17	2.60	8.92
Ontario	.76	2.23	1.38	2.58	.41	.94	3.08	12.05

Quebec's lower per capita revenues are mainly due to marked differences in the sums obtained through automobile taxes and succession duties. Automobile tax rates per motor vehicle registered were 40 per cent higher in Quebec than Ontario, but Ontario had three times as many motor vehicles per thousand of population.[13] Succession duty rates in the two provinces were similar as were corporation tax rates, so the differences here relate to the greater per capita wealth in Ontario.[14]

The contrast in public finance is far more dramatic when the per capita revenue and expenditure of Toronto and Montreal are compared.

Per Capita Expenditure in Dollars – Montreal and Toronto (1926)[15]

	Schools	Health	Social Services	Parks	Public Libraries	Total All Services
Montreal	10.90	.43	1.29	.38	.02	39.60
Toronto	15.70	2.88	1.10	1.78	.65	54.50

Per Capita Revenue – Montreal and Toronto (1926)[16]

	Real Estate Tax	School Tax	Water Tax	Business Tax	Income Tax	Total All Revenue
Montreal	15.60	10.90	4.90	3.00	—	40.00
Toronto	19.70	16.00	6.15	4.65	3.83	54.50

Montreal's significantly lower per capita revenue was due to a combination of three factors: a lower property tax level, 4.75 per cent of valuation versus 5.72 per cent in Toronto[17]; a larger amount of tax exempt properties, 25 per cent of total valuation as against 17.5 per cent in Toronto[18]; and lower levels of direct taxes. (Toronto's higher business tax and its income tax may also be important in terms of the distribution of the tax burden between income groups but that is another question.)

Lower ordinary revenues do not wholly account for the discrepancy in per capita expenditure. Basic services also suffered from a very high level of public debt in Montreal which had to be provided for out of ordinary municipal revenues. In 1926 Montreal's debt worked out to $228 per capita against $147 in Toronto. Montreal was spending more than 25 per cent of its ordinary revenues servicing its debt while the figure for Toronto was 18 per cent.[19]

Montreal's municipal finances had long been a central issue in the city's politics. "Reform" groups had repeatedly alleged that Montreal's municipal administration was riddled with patronage and corruption. In 1910, after a Royal Commission had investigated such charges, a referendum on the creation of a Board of Control was imposed by the Provincial Government. Support for a Board of Control system was organized by a Committee of Citizens which included most of the prominent business and professional men in Montreal. Their campaign concentrated on the need to bring business-like efficiency to Montreal's civic affairs and thus eliminate patronage and extravagant administration. A positive vote in the referendum and the subsequent election of the Committee's candidates in the municipal election provided an opportunity to test the effectiveness of business government.

The one specific promise that "reform" candidates had made in 1910 was the construction of a modern water filtration plant. When in the winter of 1913-14 the new aqueduct collapsed and the city went without water for several weeks, any remaining claims to efficiency appeared ludicrous. In fact, throughout the four years of the "regime of honest men" nothing significant was accomplished. The Committee of Citizens and its candidates were fascinated with new boulevards and city beautification. They did not attack the basic financial problems of the city and certainly did not propose tax increases.[20] The election of Méderic Martin as Mayor in 1914 marked the beginning of a period in municipal politics during which issues were defined rhetorically in terms of language and class. Martin and his successors ran as French Canadians and "workers" against the English businessmen and the west end. This did not mean that any reform of the tax system was undertaken and the Provincial Government's attempt to supervise the finances of the Island of Montreal during the 1920s was equally unproductive.

Certain basic features of Montreal society worked against the prospect of efficient, financially sound municipal government. Whereas Toronto's city limits encompassed most of the settled areas of the metropolitan region, including the main upper income residential areas, the City of Montreal shared the island with a number of independent municipalities. Cities like Outremont, Westmount, and in later years, the Town of Mount Royal and Hampstead, provided their wealthy citizens with excellent services but shared no responsibility for the development of the urban core. The political separation of these communities coincided with the withdrawal of their upper class population from involvement in Montreal civic affairs. Politics in Montreal had always been affected by the division of the city into two more or less hostile linguistic groups but from 1910 onwards a number of issues sharpened this division. Politics increasingly tended to focus on emotionally charged nationalist issues which, however important in the larger sense, militated against the development of strong public interest in municipal affairs.

The reader should be reminded that the tendency of political elites to focus public attention on large simplistic issues was not unique to French Canada. In Ontario political leaders talked about imperial relations or prohibition and tried to convince their electorates that these were crucial issues. In Quebec, as in Ontario and other provinces, the game of politics was usually played at a level far removed from the real problems facing the society.[21]

The real problems facing Canadians were primarily the product of a free market economy in which the owners of capital possessed virtually unlimited powers. Labour was purchased at the lowest possible cost and the public sector was supported by minimal levels of taxation. The owners of capital were consciously or unconsciously pursuing a ruthless policy of forced capital accumulation which meant that the workers of Canada were deprived of a reasonable share of national income. While it is true that all societies undergoing rapid economic growth have developed one method or another of forcing capital accumulation, it is important to recognize that in Canada, as in other countries, the working class was required to pay the price for industrial growth without receiving much in the way of benefits, at least in the years before World War II.

The Montreal working class had to pay a particularly heavy price and when in the winter of 1929 the first effects of the Great Depression were felt the workers of Montreal began to have their endurance severely tested. No other Canadian city was subjected to the same degree of unemployment and underemployment during the 1930s. Montreal's unhappy distinction was the result of a socio-economic situation in which the working class had been trapped for more than a generation. No pretense is made that that situation has been fully mapped here, nor that further research using other forms of source material would not pay dividends in such fields as housing, welfare, sanitation, education, and working conditions. But while such studies may flesh out the situation depicted here, it is unlikely that they would soften its harsh realities.

Appendix A

MONTREAL COUNCIL OF SOCIAL AGENCIES – FAMILY BUDGET*

The Dependency and Delinquency Division of the Montreal Council of Social Agencies herewith present an interim report of the special committee appointed to study the cost of living and wages in Montreal.

The report submitted covers at the present time only the part of the Committee's work which has to do with the cost of living. Later on certain suggestions are made in respect to the question of wages, which we hope will receive the serious consideration and co-operation of the Executive Committee of the Council.

1. Personnel of the Committee

Mrs. James Eccles, Mrs. Andrew Fleming, Mrs. H. M. Jaquays, Miss Grace Towers, George B. Clarke, Esq., Chairman.

2. Method pursued

Mrs. H. M. Jaquays, Miss Grace Towers and Mrs. Andrew Fleming undertook, as a sub-committee, to study a food and clothing budget. The results were arrived at by the most careful estimating of quantities, qualities, varieties and price of food and clothing. Nothing was done by guess work, experimentation and actual pricing being carried out in every instance. Corner store prices for food were listed, as the majority of families must do their shopping in the district where they live. It is recognized that the amount for clothing represents an absolute minimum.

3. Results criticized

The original report of this sub-committee was submitted to the most expert criticism of dietitians, and to the criticism of members of all divisions of the Council. The full report in its finally amended form is attached as Schedule A.

*   Source: Canada, House of Commons Select Standing Committee on Industrial and International Relations, Ottawa 1928.

Department of Labour – Canada
Typical Weekly Expenditure of a Family of Five Persons

RETAIL PRICES.

YEAR 1921

Total Expenses

ARTICLES	Quantities consumed per week	Hull	Montreal	Quebec	Sherbrooke	Average in 60 cities in Canada in 1920
Sirloin steak	2 lbs	68.6	70.2	69.2	62.8	71.2
Medium chuck	2 lbs	40.6	42.6	43.6	32.9	44.4
Veal forequarter	1 lb.	22.4	22.5	26.1	19.7	26.9
Mutton roasting hindquarter	1 lb	31.1	30.5	31.9	25.8	30.8
Pork fresh, roasting	1 lb	32.9	32.9	34.9	31.5	36.0
Pork salt	2 lbs	57.8	58.8	68.2	56.7	71.4
Bacon best smoked	1 lb	48.2	48.2	54.5	46.1	58.4
Lard	2 lbs	43.4	45.8	59.4	47.7	67.8
Eggs new-laid	1 doz	38.2	33.5	55.0	50.7	85.2
Eggs storage	1 doz	35.1	30.8	50.6	46.6	75.7
Milk	6 pts	78.6	81.0	90.6	80.4	93.0
Butter dairy, tub	2 lbs	63.0	65.0	106.2	81.2	113.4
Cheese Canadian, old	1 lb	34.8	36.8	39.0	35.4	39.2
Cheese Canadian, new	1 lb	28.2	30.6	37.7	32.0	37.5
Bread, white	15 lbs	121.5	123.0	127.5	118.5	132.0
Flour strong baker's	10 lbs	63.0	64.0	66.0	58.0	68.0
Rolled oats	5 lbs	36.0	30.0	34.0	30.5	36.0

Apples evaporated	1 lb	21.3	21.1	22.9	21.6	24.9
Prunes medium	1 lb	20.0	18.3	21.4	18.2	25.3
Sugar, granulated	4 lbs	44.4	50.0	50.4	41.2	51.2
Sugar, yellow	2 lbs	21.0	24.0	24.0	19.6	24.6
Tea, black	¼ lb	13.7	13.8	14.3	13.6	14.5
Tea, green	¼ lb	14.9	14.9	15.7	15.1	15.7
Coffee	¼ lb	13.7	13.7	14.4	13.5	14.8
Potatoes	2 gallons	35.9	36.6	57.4	64.4	75.5
Vinegar, white wine	⅛ pt	.9	.9	1.0	1.0	.9
Total for food		10.59	10.78	12.60	11.01	13.74
Starch laundry	½lb	4.4	4.5	4.7	4.4	4.9
Coal anthracite	ton	110.9	109.9	118.4	110.1	125.0
Coal bituminous	ton	75.6	77.6	86.4	73.5	92.1
Wood hard, best	cord	87.4	87.9	88.3	83.6	90.5
Wood soft,	cord	62.5	64.6	65.9	61.1	69.0
Coal oil	1 gallon	33.7	36.3	38.8	31.9	40.3
Total of fuel and light		3.70	3.76	3.98	3.60	4.17
Rent		6.83	6.77	7.62	6.89	6.60
Total 1921		21.178	21.368	24.246	21.542	24.664
Total 1920		21.994	22.387	24.161	21.226	25.635
Total 1919		18.830	18.960	22.010	18.832	22.28
Total 1918		17.027	18.128	20.935	18.785	20.67
Total 1917		15.571	16.928	19.010	16.556	18.15
Total 1916		13.143	14.548	16.253	14.209	14.78
Total 1915		11.406	12.946	13.344	12.159	13.85
Total 1914		12.217	13.604	13.172	12.296	14.31
Total 1913		12.110	13.834	12.968	12.253	14.03

4. Comments on Schedule A

The minimum figure is $1,101.76 per annum, or $91.81 per month. However, it must be noted that this total is only arrived at by deliberately excluding from the budget all provision for the following items:

(a) *Health Expenditures,* i.e., examination of teeth, medical examination, or the alternative provision for

(b) *Doctors' or dentists' fees,* medicines, etc. The Committee went on the assumption that the family was an independent working class family, which was not expected to have to depend on charitable service of any kind, but elimination of all health or sickness allowance would force it to seek the service of charitable agencies, particularly in the event of a birth or death in the family.

(c) *Higher Life Expenditure, i.e.* Life insurance, Christmas or birthday gifts to members of the family, union dues, church and charity, books and magazines, postage and stationery.

(d) *Luxuries.* Amusements of any kind at all, tobacco, candy.

(e) *Household utensils.* The original budget included a nominal sum for this purpose, but it was considered by experts to be so inadequate that it was thought better to leave it out altogether, merely calling attention to the fact that there was absolutely no provision in the budget for the replacement of china, tinware, towels or bedding.

Comparison with other Budgets

The Labour Gazette, published monthly by the Department of Labour at Ottawa, gives the budget for a family of five each month. For the month of January, 1926, the Labour Gazette's yearly budget works out as follows:

Food	$604.76
Fuel and Light	178.88
Rent	240.00
	$1,023.64

The Labour Gazette, however, gives no figures for clothing, water, etc., but indicates that the three items listed will be found to be about 65 per cent of the necessary expenditure of the average family.

Therefore, if this $1,023.64 is 65 per cent of the total, the annual expenditure will be $1,574.80 or $131.23 per month, which in terms of wages means a required wage of 58 cents per hour, 9 hours per day, 300 days in the year, as against a required wage of 41 cents an hour, 9 hours per day, 300 days a year, to produce our minimum of $1,101.76 per annum.

We do not suggest that the Labour Gazette is wrong, or that we are right, but merely wish to call attention to the discrepancy, to show that if we have erred, it has been on the side of underestimating rather than overestimating the cost of a working class family budget. The rate per hour required to produce the given totals has been worked out on a 9 hour day, and not on the regulation 8 hour day accepted at the Geneva convention by the after-war conference, because as will be shown later, the nine hour day is more common in Montreal than the eight hour day. The 300 day year will be recognized as a very generous estimate of the number of days' work during which the average day worker is employed.

The Study of Wages

The returns to date on wages paid, made by social agencies, have been small in number, and of little significance, and we feel that that is not the right way to go about this part of our study.

We want to be quite open and frank with the employers of labour in this matter. We commenced the study with the authority of the Executive Committee of the Council because we questioned in our minds as to whether all the problems of sickness, poverty, and delinquency were not in part, at least, attributable to insufficiency of income.

We believe we have made a study of the cost of living for a family of five, which is ultra-conservative in its estimates, and which any employer who gives it careful consideration will readily agree is ultra-conservative, and represents a scale below which no family could maintain its industrial efficiency or social normality.

Yet we should point out that even this conservative estimate is higher than the scale of relief given to its dependent families by the Family Welfare Association. Is it higher or lower than the incomes of thousands of working class married men? The employers of labour can most accurately and quickly answer this question.

We urge the Executive Committee of the Council to take steps at once to approach the Board of Trade, or the Manufacturers Association, laying this report before them, and asking them to give us the facts as to wages paid.

Some indication of the answer which may be expected will be found in these facts.

City labourers are paid in Montreal at the present time, i.e. April 1926:

	Per Hour	Day	Annual Income
Labourers	0 35	10 hrs.	$1,050
Helpers to blacksmiths and electricians	0 40	9 hrs.	1,080
Builders' labourers	0 40	10 hrs.	1,200
Blacksmiths and machinists	0 60	9 hrs.	1,620
Cement finishers, electricians and carpenters	0 65	9 hrs.	1,755
Steam fitters, plumbers, stone cutters	0 75	8 hrs.	1,800
Bricklayers	1 00	44 hr. week	2,288

The estimated annual incomes are based on the bold assumption that all these people work 300 days per year.

Above we have dealt with workers who are in large per cent of their· total number seasonally engaged, hence their incomes are actually very much less than the figures given.

If we turn to another group of workers altogether, people who are more likely to be employed on a weekly or monthly basis, and employed throughout the year, such as warehouse men, janitors, watchmen, etc., we find that the wages vary from $15 to $22 per week, i.e. $780 to $1,144 per annum, on the basis of a 52 week year; it will be noted that 1 and 2 of the above list and these weekly wage employees even on this basis will receive less than our minimum budget.

Respectfully submitted.

Chairman.

Secretary.

COST OF LIVING SCHEDULE A

Budget for Man, Wife, and Three Children, Girl of 13, Boys, 11 and 9 years

SUMMARY FOR THE YEAR

	Month	Year
Housing (4 rooms)	$18 00	$216 00
Fuel	44 00	528 00
Fuel, light and gas	7 55	90 60
Clothing	15 20	182 40
Water tax	1 08	12 96
Car fares	3 65	43 80
Newspaper	0 50	6 00
School books	1 00	12 00
Soap	0 83⅓	10 00
	$91 81⅓	$1,101 76

Weekly Allotment		Corner Store Prices
Milk and Cheese –	cts.	$ cts.
14 qts. milk	14	1 96
½ lb. cheese	25	12½
Eggs and Meat –		
3 lbs. round steak	20	60
3 lbs. corn beef	22	66
2 lbs. haddock	12½	25
1 lb. liver	30	30
1 doz. eggs	45	45
Vegetables –		
4 lbs. carrots	3	12
2 lbs. turnips	3	6
2 lbs. onions	5	10
12 lbs. potatoes	2½	30
2 tins tomatoes	10	20
Fruit –		
6 oranges	30	15
18 apples	30	30
1 lb. prunes	12½	12½
1 lb. figs	12½	12½
¼ lb. raisins or currants	16	4
Bread and Cereals –		
14 lvs. bread	12	1.68
2 lbs. flour	7	14
1 lb. macaroni	8	8
1 lb. rice	9	9
½ lb. cornmeal	6	3
3½ lbs. oatmeal	6	21
¼ lb. sago	10	2½
¼ lb. tapioca	10	2½
¼ lb. barley	10	2½
½ lb. split peas	10	5
¼ lb. beans	9	2½
2 lbs. sugar	7	14
Sweets –		
1 lb. jam	12½	12½
½ lb. corn syrup	9	4½
Fats –		
1½ lbs. butter	46	69
4 lb. lard	21	21
½ lb. suet	18	9
½ lb. cocoa	16	8
1 tin peanut butter	25	25
¼ lb. tea	60	15
¼ pkg. cornstarch	12	3
¼ pkg. baking powder	32	4
¼ tin pepper	9	2¼
¼ bag salt	10	2¼
		$10.14

MENUS FOR ONE WEEK AS PER ALLOTMENT

Monday

Breakfast. – Large bowl of porridge, sugar, 2 slices of bread each, butter, 1 cup of milk per child, tea and ¼ cup of milk per adult. Repeat.

Dinner—1½ lbs. round steak in stew, dumplings, tomatoes, cornstarch pudding and jam.

Tea – 5 boiled eggs, ½ lb. stewed prunes, 2 slices of bread each, milk and tea as above.

Tuesday

Dinner – 3 lbs. corn beef, carrots, 10 potatoes; corncake made from 1 egg, ½ cup of milk, sugar, salt, lard, cornmeal, white flour; corn syrup, milk and tea as above.

Tea – Pea soup with water beef was boiled in and 1 cup of peas, i.e. ½ lb.; 2 slices of bread each, baked apples, milk and tea as above.

Wednesday

Dinner – Cold corned beef, carrots, 10 potatoes, 1 slice of bread each, rice pudding from ½ cup of rice, 4½ cups milk, sugar.

Tea – Macaroni and cheese, with 1 cup of milk; cocoa 2½ cups of milk, 1 cup of water; currant buns, from 2 cups of flour, water, sugar, currants, baking powder, lard; 2 slices of bread each, jam, tea and ¼ cup of milk per adult.

Thursday

Dinner – 1½ lbs. round steak minced, ¼ cup of boiled rice, 1 turnip, suet pudding from flour, suet, raisins, baking powder, ½ cup of milk, with corn syrup, 1 slice of bread each.

Tea – Fried potatoes, 2 slices of bread each, stewed figs, 1 cup of milk per child, tea and ¼ cup of milk per adult.

Friday

Dinner – 2 lbs. haddock fried in lard, potatoes, onions, tapioca or sago pudding, from ¼ lb. sago, 4½ cups of milk; 1 slice of bread each.

Tea – 5 boiled eggs, 2 slices of bread each, stewed apples, milk and tea as above.

Saturday

Dinner – Tomatoes and macaroni, potatoes, cottage pudding from ½ cup of milk, 1 egg, flour, lard, baking powder, 1 slice of bread each.

Tea – Bean soup from 7 cups of milk and beans; 2 slices of bread, cheese, butter, jam, ¼ cup of milk and tea for adults.

Sunday

Dinner – 1 lb. liver baked, onions, potatoes; rolly-poly from suet, milk and water, flour, sugar; 1 slice of bread each.

Tea – Barley and vegetable soup, with 1 cup of milk; 2 slices of bread each, stewed prunes, 1 cup of milk per child, tea and ¼ cup of milk per adult.

NOTES – 14 quarts of milk per week, 2 quarts per day, 10 cups. Loaf of bread equals 17 slices, ½ inch thick. Average price given for potatoes, eggs and butter. Other cheap meats are tripe, pork and beans, salt cod cooked in milk, fresh herring, tommy cod, beef kidney, stewing mutton, stewing veal.

Clothing Budget		PER YEAR
MAN	$ cts.	$ cts.
1 cap (2 years)	0 69	
1 felt hat (2 years)	1 25	0 97
1 overcoat (2 years)	10 50	5 25
1 rubber coat (2 years)	6 00	3 00
1 suit (2 years)	12 95	6 47½
1 sweater (2 years)	4 00	2 00
3 working shirts	0 69	2 07
2 white shirts	1 00	2 00
1 pair pants	1 89	1 89
2 collars	0 17½	0 35
2 pair overalls	1 89	3.78
1 tie	0 35	0 35
6 handkerchiefs	0 06¼	0 37½
6 pair hose	0 50	3 00
1 pair gloves	0 79	0 79
1 pair mittens	0 50	0 50
2 pair shoes	3 45	6 90
2 pair summer underwear	0 69	0 69
2 pair winter underwear	1 55	3 10
2 pair pyjamas	1 25	2 50
1 pair braces	0 90	0 90
1 pair garters	0 20	0 20
2 pair rubbers	0 50	1 00
1 tooth brush	0 40	0 40
Repairs to shoes	2 50	2 50
		50 99
WOMAN		
2 hats	1 00	2 00
1 winter coat (3 years)	12 00	4 00
1 rubber coat (2 years)	6 00	3 00
1 serge dress	5 00	5 00
2 wash dresses	1 75	3 50
3 aprons	0 75	2 25

6 handkerchiefs	0 10	0 60
6 pair stockings	0 59	3 34
2 summer vests	0 39	0 78
2 summer knickers	0 59	1 18
2 winter vests	0 59	1 18
2 winter knickers	0 79	1 58
1 pr. wool gloves	0 83	0 83
1 pr. rubbers	0 50	0 50

CANADIAN BROTHERHOOD OF RAILWAY EMPLOYEES MINIMUM HEALTH AND DECENCY BUDGET*

This budget was constructed so as to serve in laying down a standard of living suitable for wage earners in all parts of the country, irrespective of racial origin. The principal guide was that these workers and their families live and work in America, and if they have not already, are quickly assuming an American mode of living. This has been accepted as a proper guide and principal in our Canadian study and applied with the necessary local modifications.

Localities Chosen

The following centres were chosen by the Executive Committee of the Brotherhood for the study of the cost of living in Canada. These were chosen on the principle of one each, of a large, medium and small urban centre; as those in which railroad workers reside and work; as those which are principally railroad points on Canadian National lines, and on which Brotherhood members are employed. These cities are believed also to serve as guides for the cost of a minimum health and decency standard of living in each of the provinces in which these cities are located.

Localities Chosen	Population
Maritime Provinces:	1921 Census
Sydney, N.S.	22,545
Truro, N.S.	7,562
Moncton, N.B.	17,488
Central Provinces:	
Toronto, Ont.	521,893
Belleville, Ont.	12,206
Montreal, Que.	618,506
Coteau Jct., Que	
Western Provinces:	
Winnipeg, Man.	179,087
Saskatoon, Sask.	25,739
Kamloops, B.C.	4,501

* Source Canada, House of Commons Select Standing Committee on Industrial and International Relations, Ottawa 1928, p. 83.

The investigation was conducted during the spring, summer and fall of 1925, lasting from March 9 to November 12. Prices were secured in the "personal shopping" method. The stores in seven of the above named cities were visited by the writer.[1] The findings and the method of procedure follow below:—

Average Cost of Minimum Health and Decency Budget in Canada

Summary of Family Budget for Worker's Family of Five Persons

I. Food		639 04
II. Clothing:		
Husband	$118 70	
Wife	147 60	
Boy, 12 years	83 21	
Girl, 6 years	65 14	
Boy, 2 years	8 26	452 91
III. Household Equipment	$979 93	
7 per cent annual upkeep		68 59
IV. Rent, Light and heat		565 30
V. Cleaning Supplies, etc.		44 10
VI. Miscellaneous		432 43
Total		$2,202 37

Method of Investigation

On arriving at each city the following procedure was carried out:

1. A tour of the city to become acquainted with the character of each residential section; ascertaining the class of people resident in each, the types of housing, and local shop services. Establishing the workers' section.

2. Classifying the stores. Ascertaining which ones in the business or downtown section are patronized by working people; which sell reliable, medium-priced goods; which specialize in "fancy" or "job-lot" goods; ascertaining to what extent departmental or small stores have wage-earners' custom; ascertaining to what extent workers' wives shop in their local stores, and which of these carry full and medium-grade, medium-priced stock of wares; ascertain to what extent the cash-and-carry or credit system of buying prevails.

3. Classifying municipal services. Ascertaining what hospital, dispensary and other medical services exist, and to what extent these are available free, or partially free of charge, to working people, and to what extent these are used. Ascertaining what recreational facilities are available, playgrounds for children, parks, clubs, community houses, social and athletic associations.

4. Classifying amusement and educational facilities; theatres, libraries, churches, schools, lodges, museums, etc.

5. Ascertaining local methods of transport, lighting, heating and cooking fuel.

B. *Pricing the Budget.*—Having become acquainted with the sections of the city and the stores, the following were eliminated:

(1) *Stores:* Bargain-sale or "job-lot" stores; which did not appear to have a permanent character; stores which catered only to the very poorest people; stores which did not carry a reliable class of goods. The five-and-ten-cent stores; stores which sacrificed quality to maintain low prices; stores which did not have working class custom.

(2) *Houses:* Only those houses which stood in well-cared for, respectable working class districts and which contained all the conveniences which conformed to the building laws and requirements of sanitation, health and decency, were chosen. Houses in the slum districts or near factories or railway tracks were not included.

Five quotations from five separate stores were obtained for each item on the budget. No price was obtained over the telephone or by mail. The writer visited each store, personally examined the commodity to be priced. Prices were not taken from irresponsible salespeople. In the department stores, prices were secured from either, managers of departments, buyers, or from those clerks which were appointed by the manager to render this service. In the small stores prices were obtained from the proprietor direct. In all cases, with only two exceptions in one eastern city, this service was rendered with interested attention and helpful guidance.

The following order was observed in pricing the items:—

1. *Food*—Meats, fish, groceries, fruits and vegetables were priced in the separate stores specializing in these goods: meat at the butcher stores, fish at the fish store, etc. In the choice of grocery stores, it was found advantageous both from the point of view of economy in time and choice of goods, to select the grocery store which stocked both groceries and fruits and vegetables. On checking the prices, it was found that the prices did not vary here from the fruiterer's. Prices were also obtained from the vegetable truck-dealer. Care was had to establish and price the same grade, make, size, at all stores, and a great deal of difficulty was experienced in this task.

Food of a medium quality was selected. Quotations on medium-quantities, such as a family of five would purchase, were taken. Cash and not credit prices were asked for. Extra charges for delivery services were ascertained. "Sale" prices were not considered.

2. *Clothing.*—Prices were obtained from departmental stores, reliable ladies' wear stores, from men's clothing and haberdashers, from children's clothing, and boot and hat or millinery stores. Garments of a medium-grade, of reliable make, which promised durability and true economy, were selected. Only standard prices were taken; bargain-sales, or "special" priced goods were disregarded. In those stores which stocked exclusive wear, the more moderate grades were selected. As a rule, the principal guide to the practical quality were those garments designated usually as "best sellers"; the ordinary citizen's and practical working person's choice. Both the choice of stores and the selection of articles were checked up by interviewing workers and their wives, as well as other representative citizens of the city.

3. *Housing.*—Quotations on working class homes in working class districts were secured, together with the street and number of each house, from local reliable and established realtors. Having this, a personal visit to each house quoted on, was paid; each was in turn inspected, by the good will of the tenants residing there. In addition, an extensive independent inquiry, street by street, of selected representative houses, was made from the people living in them. From this inquiry and investigation was gained: (1) the rent of the house; (2) an inspection of the type of house; (3) the amount of fuel burned and the annual cost of same; (4) the amount and cost of lighting, and cooking fuel, as well as the type of cooking and heating appliances and methods; (5) water rates, and other taxes.

4. *Household Equipment.*—The budget allows only a very modest type of furniture and furnishings. This of course is not easy to select, for here as in clothing, the range of style, make, quality, and personal taste is wide. Therefore again the "best sellers," the goods purchased by the average citizen were relied upon. In this also great care had to be exercised. Many workers indulge in chesterfield suites, victrolas, in radios, in sunparlors. In the last years there have risen vogues in kinds of wood and workmanship. The choice for this budget was:

(a) For the living room: oak, leather-covered armchairs, a davenport to match, with the purpose in mind that this can be used to supply an extra bed-room when necessary; an oak library table, and an inexpensive standard-size floor rug.

(b) For the dining room: a simple, medium-priced oak dining room suite of eight pieces; a set of six diners, an extension table, and a buffet. For the floor, a congoleum rug.

(c) For the kitchen: A coal range; a 48-inch pine table, two chairs, and a full range of kitchen utensils, of economical and lower priced grades (*i.e.,* grey enamel pots).

(d) For the bedrooms: Modern steel beds, oak furniture of simple but durable make; rag carpets; medium quality, durable and economical bed furnishings.

... These items are presumed to have been purchased as the home was organized by the family. They constitute what has been agreed upon as being necessary equipment for a family of five persons, living in health and decency. The budget allows only for 7 per cent annual upkeep cost on such equipment.

As will be noted, there are no provisions for such sundries as curtains, window shades, etc. These items are to be supplied somehow from the possible savings in the home economy.

Local Purchasing Conditions

With minor exceptions all of the commodities listed on the budget were found in stock in the stores and in demand by the custom. These exceptions were not in the realm of food, and clothing, but in household equipment—for instance, some western stores did not stock dish drainers, though they did have bridge tables.

Houses in urban centres do not vary to any great degree; and it was comparatively easy to secure the rent of a standard five or six-roomed house containing the standard conveniences.

The important variations were found in local methods of heating, the kind of fuel used, and in the kinds of cooking fuel locally available. Throughout electricity was the mode of lighting the home.

Further variations were made in the choice of underclothing and top clothing for the winter months; in the western cities those of heavier make were selected.

On the whole it was found that the items listed in the budget were those which are to-day the most standardized in manufacture and in distribution in all parts of the country. The large department stores, the mail-order houses, the jobbers, the travelling salesmen from the large central business houses, the staple manufactures, and national advertising have made the procurance of a standard budget such as this is, not an ideal, but a reality and actuality. It is not a question now whether these articles are being bought by working people and their families, but whether they are bought in sufficient quantities to allow them to live in health and decency. The fact that these articles are for sale everywhere in quantities, that they are considered as standard and ordinary stock, shows that these are purchased and are in demand. To repeat: the question is how many workers' families can and do buy these items in sufficient quantities and in the order of their necessities, and not luxuries, was seen by the writer when she was told by the proprietor of an ambitious store serving a working class community: "We don't take much stock of these goods you are interested in; they are common— we don't make much money on them—they are too standardized." The same was experienced in the clothing and furniture stores.

Appendix B

Quebec Royal Commission on Tuberculosis, 1909: Conclusions of an Enquiry into the Causes of Quebec's High Rate of Tuberculosis

Conclusions of the Enquiry

This enquiry carried on by means of a medical referendum, that is to say, among those who are in a better position to be familiar with the subject under consideration, has revealed the following positive facts:

1. Official statistics inform us only of the minimum extent of the disease, for they give only the duly recorded deaths and not the number of all who suffer more or less from it. But, even if we consider only the number of deaths, we have reason to be anxious, for it represents too large a number of losses of life that might have been avoided. If we were to see a city such as Three Rivers, for instance, with its population of 20,000, disappear in a decade, the entire population of the province would be horrified by such a calamity. As a matter of fact tuberculosis has taken from us 33,190 lives in a decade.

2. Our women die in greater numbers, contrary to what happens in other countries. Why? Because our women do not pay attention to following the rules of hygiene in domestic life: because, especially, they do not take proper precautions before and after confinement; because before becoming mothers, a too great number of our girls are etiolated or withered from work in factories.

3. Mortality is greater among French-Canadians than among English-Canadians, because they are more exposed to industrial labor and other fatiguing work; because they live in more or less unhealthy, crowded buildings; because they are more ignorant of and observe in a lesser degree general hygiene; because the idea that tuberculosis is hereditary is still ingrained in them and they do not take the necessary precautions against contagion.

4. Immigration, which has assumed greater proportions during

the past few years, throws, into the metropolis especially, thousands of people, who, owing to their slight means, lodge in any kind of a house, with one or two families in a room; live in disgusting uncleanliness, and by nourishing morbid germs, contribute also to make their quarters real hot-beds of the disease. Most of those immigrants are nomadic, frequently moving from house to house, ward to ward, city to city, therefore spreading the contagion and rendering their cognizance by the health authorities very difficult. Moreover, being ignorant of our health regulations and laws, they frequently infringe them and are a bad example to the population who are already difficult to educate in this matter. The law which allows of their being deported within two years of their arrival if they become tuberculous, is of delusive efficiency because the health authorities are not sufficiently equipped to exercise adequate supervision.

5. Contagion plays the principal part among causes of tuberculization in our families, both in the country and in town. It has ample opportunities, for people generally are ignorant of the infectious nature of the disease. Unhealthy dwellings come next.

6. The unhealthy conditions found in our dwellings both in the country and in town are in order of their importance, lack of ventilation, lack of sunlight, overcrowding of bedrooms, dampness and faulty heating.

7. There are also many lodgings infected by consumptives which, through lack of disinfection, convey the disease to healthy people.

8. In all places where people are gathered together such as workshops, offices, factories, schools, colleges, convents, asylums, prisons, etc., the danger of tuberculous contagion exists owing to the lack of precaution against it, due to the ignorance of the contagious nature of tuberculosis or the negligence of employers or the heads of public offices or great companies.

9. A great many teachers of both sexes, especially among the religious orders, are tuberculous, and a danger to their pupils.

10. The pupils in elementary schools are attacked more by glandular tuberculosis and tuberculosis of the bones and contagion from pupil to pupil is rather limited. Nevertheless some pupils have open tuberculosis and a single one may contaminate many.

11. The majority of the schools in the province do not give each pupil 150 cubic feet of air space and this figure is a barely acceptable minimum. Americans exact more: 200 feet at least and recommend 250. Thus, our schools are overcrowded.

12. The majority of the schools in the province have no appliances for ventilation. Ventilation is provided solely by

windows and does not count in winter, since the windows are continually and hermetically closed. The chief defect in our schools is lack of ventilation.

13. Tuberculosis among our children is chiefly due to family contagion and to a slight extent to infection by milk.

14. The chief predisposing causes of tuberculosis in children are living continually in vitiated air at home or at school; faulty feeding during the first months, which produces rickets and general debilitation; lack of proper attention after infectious diseases, especially measles and whooping cough; the presence in a great many of infected tonsils and adenoid tumours.

15. Our milch cows are tuberculous in the proportion of about 10% and the infection of the child by milk is duly established by physicians.

16. Our cities do not present the same degree nor the same elements of unhealthiness. Among all, Montreal is the most unhealthy, owing to the atmosphere always full of dust raised by automobiles and tramway cars, of smoke from the chimneys of its numerous factories; to its many unhealthy dwellings; to its considerable population of immigrants who huddle together in dirty, infected and damp lodgings and in quarters that are unhealthy by their age; the crowding of houses together and narrow streets. In other cities that element of unhealthiness, immigration, does not exist.

17. The chief cause of tuberculosis in the country is family contagion due to ignorance of the contagious nature of the disease. The consequence of such ignorance is that people take no precautions against the infection, they expectorate on the ground or floor, infect their dwellings and do not isolate their sick, live in immediate contact with them, their children sharing the same room and even the same bed with them. Girls who have left home to go and work in the cities either as servants or in factories come back with the disease and spread contagion. Moreover, there are very powerful predisposing causes in our country people's manner of living; they live continually in an atmosphere vitiated through non-renewal of air, they shut their windows to the sunlight, make their bed-rooms too small and overcrowd them.

18. In industry, the law does not as yet contain any provision respecting operatives in an advanced stage of tuberculosis and there is no medical inspection of industrial establishments. Now, there is contagion between people working together. The law requires that spittoons be placed in workshops, but a great many employers are ignorant of such necessity and even of the law. Mechanical ventilation, so necessary in certain trades producing

GENERAL MORTALITY RATE, MONTREAL AND TORONTO

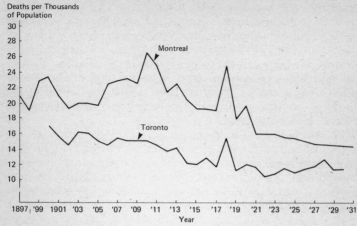

Source: Montreal — Annual Report of the Montreal Board of Health, 1900-1930

Toronto — Report of the Registrar General, Ontario
Sessional Papers, 1900-1930

INFANT MORTALITY, MONTREAL AND TORONTO

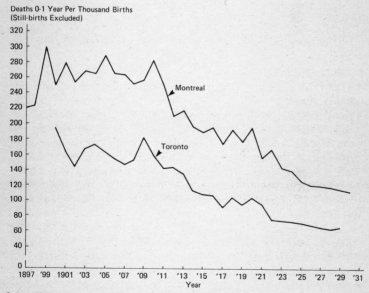

Source: Montreal — Annual Report of the Montreal Board of Health, 1900-1930

Toronto — Report of the Registrar General, Ontario
Sessional Papers, 1900-1930

metallic, mineral, vegetable or organic dust, is lacking in a great many factories. Means of securing personal cleanliness among operatives are also lacking in several factories. The protective laws are perhaps sufficient, but the staff of inspectors and supervisors is not numerous enough and, above all, there is a lack of competent medical men, expert in hygiene, for hitherto more thought has been devoted to the prevention of accidents than to the prevention of diseases from industrial centres. In all our cities where there are factories, there is one great cause of the etiolation of youth predisposing to tuberculosis, and that is premature or excessive labor.

19. Alcoholism with its consequences: degeneration of the individual and of his progeny; straitened circumstances or poverty – exists more in certain parts of our province than in others. Nevertheless, it does not play an immoderate and almost preponderant part here as in France. It certainly has however, its share of responsibility in causing tuberculosis in our Province.

THE ORGANIZATION OF THE GOUTTES DE LAIT*

Extract of a report submitted to the Board of Health, by request, concerning the means to be adopted to reduce infantile mortality. This report was divided into "Permanent and Provisional" organizations of which the principal recommendations were as follows:

Provisional Organization. – (Admitting of being applied this year.)

After consultations with several authorities on pediatrics such as Dr. Sévérin Lachapelle, of the Medical Faculty of Laval and one of the organizers of "La Goutte de Lait" (parish of l'Enfant Jésus), Dr. Blackadder, of the Medical Faculty of McGill; Dr. Elzéar Pelletier, secretary of the Provincial Board of Health, and other medical men on the question of founding a permanent organization for teaching mothers the care to be given to babies with a view to reducing mortality among them, it was unanimously acknowledged that such an organization was impracticable this year. The only measures to be taken for the present were the founding of more numerous "Gouttes de Lait" establishments on the same principle as those already existing, namely, "The Montreal Foundling Hospital," "l'Enfant Jésus" and the "St. Justine Hospital," whose work has given good results: the donating of a sum of at least $500 to each of these local stations to pay rents, salaries of nurses, milk, bottles, etc., for a period of

* From the *Annual Report*, Montreal Board of Health, 1911, pp. 12-19.

four months, presumably from June 1st to October 1st. The great difficulty was in deciding on the proper localities for these stations and the number required to meet the demands of the poorer population the number of whom is at present merely conjectural. The only way to settle this point was to take the total number of deaths from diarrhaeal complaints in each ward and to install "Gouttes de Lait" stations in those wards where such deaths were the most numerous.

The three stations already in existence received the following sums:

1. – The Montreal Foundling and Baby Hospital, 43 Argyle Avenue, St. Andrew ward $500.00
2. – L'Enfant Jésus Dispensary, Laurier ward 1,000.00
3. – St. Justine Hospital, 1107 De Lorimier Avenue, De Lorimier ward 1,000.00

The following localities are especially recommended for those wards where infant mortality is the highest: –

The twelve proposed "Gouttes de Lait" stations:
1. – St. Justine Hospital, 773a Lagauchetière Street East, near Plessis, in Papineau ward 500.00
2. – St. Jean-Baptiste Parish, Rachel and Sanguinet Streets, St. Jean-Baptiste ward . . . 500.00
3. – St. Joseph's Parish, Richmond Street, St. Joseph ward 500.00
4. – St. Denis ward, corner Beaubien and St. Denis 500.00
5. – St. Henry ward, at the old City Hall 500.00
6. – St. Cunegonde ward 500.00
7. – St. Lawrence ward, 161 Dorchester west, near St. George Street 500.00
8. – Hochelaga ward 500.00
9. – St. Mary ward 500.00
10. – Duvernay ward 500.00
11. – St. Gabriel ward 500.00
12. – St. James ward 500.00

$6,000.00

I would recommend that the City Council appropriate the sum of $6,000.00 to cover the cost of these twelve "Gouttes de Lait" stations. At the same time, I would suggest that a contract be passed by virtue of which those in charge of these establishments be submitted to and act in conformity with a Medical Bureau composed of the Medical Health Officer and some specialists in puericulture, this would give a moral support to the establishments and make them more popular with people of all nationalities.

After advising with Drs. Blackadder and Lachapelle, we adopted the necessary measures to be put into force during this season. These gentlemen have generously consented, in the interest of public health, to act as directors of this movement during the present year. I would, therefore, respectfully recommend that the services so graciously offered by these men be accepted and that they be named as members of the Board of Directors, thus officially recognizing their authority. Their assistance as specialists in puericulture will be of great value in arranging the details of a permanent organization. As these gentlemen are present, I would ask them to give their views on this important subject as they can do so much better than I can.

Dr. Lachapelle gave it as his opinion that only nurses specially trained in puericulture should be employed in instructing mothers in the care of their new born infants. Six months would be ample to train these nurses sufficiently for this work. At present in the "Gouttes de Lait" station of l'Enfant Jésus parish, mothers were being instructed in these matters by some ladies who, despite their devotion and good will, possessed no knowledge of puericulture.

Permanent Organizations.

To educate mothers so that they may be enabled to prevent such accidents as are likely to occur during gestation; to advise them of the best means to increase the flow of milk for the nourishment of their babies. All specialists in pediatrics are aware that ignorance on the part of mothers in the matter of hygiene and the care of the newly born is the chief cause of infantile mortality and still-births. Speaking practically, the care taken by mothers of themselves and of their babies should not be left entirely to their own maternal instincts and love. Rather they should trust to scientific and experienced advice. This part of modern education, or puericulture has been very much neglected up to the present. If such education were more general, it is presumable that the most important duty of mothers in regard to their own health and that of their children would not be so often neglected for the sake of fashion or the habits of modern society. Feeding babies at the maternal breast is insisted on by all competent authorities both from a scientific and a moral standpoint. The new born infant has an absolute right to the natural milk of its mother and it is her duty to nourish her child at her breast, it is the only way to activate the secretion of milk and to insure her baby's life.

How is such an education to be given? By lectures, discussions or conferences, by circulars, pamphlets or the public press; by lessons in schools and especially by teaching puericulture more extensively in medical faculties; by schools for mothers, by exhibitions, by free medical consultations in dispensaries and above all by house to house visits to young mothers by competent nurses acting under the direction of a medical council. The help of all who possess a certain authority in society such as clergymen, doctors, public educationalists and philanthropists, would be of great assistance. Once public confidence gained, the physician would not be sent for so often at the last stage of a disease, but rather at its inception.

Food.

Pure milk sterilized or pasteurized. In cases where mothers, on the advice of medical men, cannot nurse their infants themselves and when no wet-nurse is procurable, recourse should be had to the "Gouttes de Lait" dispensaries. For the past few years the parish of l'Enfant Jésus, the St. Justine and the Montreal Foundling and Baby hospitals have had great success with their "Gouttes de Lait" establishments and for this reason parishes or local depots which can furnish pure milk should receive the greatest encouragement. Trained nurses should visit the homes of newly born babies also and give all the advice possible to parents, teaching them the special precautions to be taken in cases of illness. These children should be taken to the dispensaries for medical examination at least once a week.

I am informed that the milk used at these "Gouttes de Lait" establishments is prepared in two ways: Ist. Homogenized milk furnished by the St. Lawrence Dairy. Homogenization is a process which consists in passing cow's milk between two agate stones whereby the globules are broken up and reduced in size, thus making an emulsion which is easily digested by infants as these globules are more proportionate in size to those of mother's milk. 2nd. Milk obtained from local dealers. These two kinds of milk are graduated in three proportions: ½ water, ⅓ water and pure milk, delivered after sterilization. Oatmeal or barley gruel is provided where the physician in attendance finds milk injurious.

Houses where infants live should be inspected carefully and in detail, any condition found prejudicial to health should be reported at once to the Board of Health. When houses are overcrowded the children should be recommended to the "Fresh Air Fund" organization or to the "King's Daughters" creche at Mount Royal Park.

Means to be employed to carry out the above programme in a practical way:

(a) Allot a few thousand dollars to enable newly born children to be watched and looked after, whether these children be of rich or poor parents, class delimitation being impossible.

(b) Pay a fee to physicians, etc., for properly reporting births. It would be well, also, if possible, that women about to be confined could be visited and advised on their condition. The old Roman law, in view of the scarcity of physicians, compelled all persons about to be married to possess a certain knowledge of obstetrics, I know of no reason why a like knowledge should not be required to-day of future husbands. It would tend very much to safeguard the lives of the newly born.

(c) Pass a law prohibiting the sale of narcotic syrups and long tubed nursing bottles.

(d) Induce municipalities to refrain from cutting off the water supply from poor families for the non-payment of taxes.

(e) Encourage the sale of pure milk by granting a special licence for the sale of milk to be used for infants, as recommended by Dr. Elzéar Pelletier. District physicians have no time to inspect houses or superintend the feeding of children, this work should be done by special employees.

(f) Competent trained nurses, the number to be determined later on, should be affiliated to the "Gouttes de Lait" for these visits. A person on reporting a birth should be given a circular or pamphlet explaining the manner of feeding and caring for the new born. The nurses could do this work and make these instructions plainer by verbal explanation.

(g) If the "Gouttes de Lait" system was carried out and nurses employed, an advisory Board of expert physicians would be named to work out details, rules, etc., and act as consultants.

(h) A general plan could be adopted and estimates prepared to aid private effort engaged in this work the same as is done in New York, Philadelphia, Boston and other cities. I would call your attention to what has already been done in New York. "The Association for the betterment of the poorer classes" which has existed for 66 years, was followed soon after by the establishment of the "Municipal Bureau of Studies", a philanthropic society which was founded for the purpose of helping in the adoption of such sanitary laws it considered necessary and seeing that these laws, when passed, be put in practice. It was through the influence of this Board that the daily birth report was obtained from the Department of Statistics for the purpose of watching over these children, one of the best means of combatting infantile mortality. In order to facilitate its work, the association formed itself into three sections:

Ist. The milk committee of New York.

2nd. A section appointed to visit homes of women recently confined and their infants.

3rd. A section appointed to look after women about to be confined.

The success of this association is beyond all doubt as is proved by the fact that in a period of 10 years infantile mortality fell from 244 per thousand to 144, nearly 100 per thousand. During a period of 25 years, the proportion of deaths of children in this city, under 1 year to the births, was 253.89 per 1000, one of the highest in North America. On the other hand, our birth-rate, as shown by our last report, was 37.15 per 1000 which is also one of the highest on the continent. If philanthropic societies interested in the welfare of children and helped by the City, obtained the same success here as in New York, out of the 14,678 children born as shown by our last report (a number not absolutely complete), we could be able to save at least 1,400.

Bibliographical Note

No purpose would be served by listing all the sources used in this study. I have tried to give complete citations in the notes. Some of the more important sources may, however, be briefly described.

PRINTED SOURCES

All of the important administrative divisions of the Quebec Government filed annual reports which are printed in the *Sessional Papers*. The Reports utilized in this study are all indexed by name in the *Sessional Papers* though the Reports of labour officials are to be found in the *Report of the Minister of Colonization* 1897-1903 and in the *Report of the Minister of Colonization and Public Works* 1903-05. After 1905 all of the bureaus concerned with labour matters reported to the Minister of Public Works and Labour.

These reports are a distillation of a vast amount of material submitted by officials of the various departments. The researcher who could locate the material on which these Annual Reports were based, such as the monthly reports of individual factory inspectors, would be able to draw a far more detailed picture of certain aspects of the society than I have presented here.

The same comment applies to the Annual Reports of the administrative departments of the City of Montreal. Health Board officials printed short summaries of the work of each division of the Board and documents such as special committee reports and draft by-laws. The working papers of the Board including material like the "Sanitary House Record" would provide a very rich source for a more detailed study of Montreal.

The *Annual Report of the Montreal Catholic School Commission* along with the *Annual Report of the Montreal Protestant School Commission* was printed in the *Report of the Superintendant of Public Instruction* (Sessional Papers) from 1897 to 1906. No further school commission reports were printed in the Sessional Papers. The *Reports* of the Protestant Commission were printed privately thereafter but the archives of the Montreal Catholic School Commission could only locate typescripts of the *Financial Report* for certain years in the period 1906-29.

The *Annual Reports* of the Montreal Charities Organization Society and after 1919 the Montreal Council of Social Agencies provide the best overview of charitable work in the anglophone sector. No such uniform body of information on the development of Catholic agencies exists and my views on Catholic welfare activities are based on the reports of a number of individual institutions which are printed in the *Report of the Inspector of Reformatories and Industrial Schools* (Sessional Papers), the *Report of the Bureau of Municipal Assistance* (Montreal Board of Health) and on the very valuable evidence presented to the Quebec Social Insurance Commission.

MONOGRAPHS

The McGill Social Research Project under the direction of Leonard C. Marsh was responsible for a number of monographs which are basic sources for the historian of the depression decade and of considerable importance for understanding the 1920s. Marsh is now remembered chiefly for his *Report on Social Security,* Ottawa 1943, the Canadian equivalent of the Beveridge Report, but his other published works, *Employment Research,* 1933, *Health and Unemployment,* 1937, and *Canadians In and Out of Work,* 1940, deserve much greater attention. A full list of the investigations proposed by the McGill project is appended to *Employment Research* but some studies were not completed. Marsh's own unpublished contribution, *The Problem of Seasonal Unemployment,* 1933, is of great value for the 1920s as is Phyllis Heaton, *Standard of Living Studies*, 1935.

Notes

Abbreviations Used in the Notes

A.R.M.B.H.	*Annual Report of the Montreal Board of Health*
A.R.Q.B.H.	*Annual Report of the Quebec Board of Health*
A.R.Q.D.L.	*Annual Report of the Quebec Department of Labour*
A.R.S.P.I.	*Annual Report of the Superintendant of Public Instruction*
M.C.O.S.	Montreal Charities Organization Society
M.C.S.C.	Montreal Catholic School Commission
P.S.C.M.	Protestant School Commission of Montreal

1 The City Below the Hill

1. Herbert Brown Ames, *The City Below the Hill* (Montreal, 1897). All quotations and statistics in this chapter are from Ames unless otherwise cited.
2. Montreal, *Report of the City Surveyor*, 1898.
3. *A.R.M.B.H.*, 1899, p. 7.
4. *Report of the City Surveyor*, 1898, p. 3.
5. *A.R.Q.B.H.*, 1902, p. 49.
6. Montreal, *Annual Report of the Superintendent of the Montreal Water Works*, 1897, p. 2.
7. Jessie Di Paulo, "The Development of Parks and Playgrounds in Montreal: 1900-1910," Appendix "B" (Unpublished B.A. Honours Essay, Loyola College, 1969).
8. F. L. Omstead, *Mount Royal* (Montreal, 1881), pp. 4-5.
9. Daniel Russell, "H. B. Ames and Municipal Reform" (Unpublished M.A. Thesis, McGill University, 1971).
10. Arthur Mann, *Yankee Reformers in the Urban Age* (New York, Harper, 1966), p. 115.
11. Ames does not define the age level that distinguished "lads" from children. Provincial law set the minimum age for boys in factories at 12, 14 for girls. This law did not apply to children employed in stores or as delivery boys.
12. Canada Census of 1901, Vol. III, pp. 232-37.
13. *Report of the City Surveyor*, 1898, p. 3.
14. *A.R.M.B.H.*, 1898, p. 6.
15. Joseph Gauvreau, "La Goutte de Lait," *L'Ecole Sociale Populaire*, No. 29 (Montreal, 1914), pp. 5, 6.

16. *A.R.Q.B.H.*, 1897, p. 36.
17. *A.R.M.B.H.*, 1899, p. 23.
18. The text of key sections of the Industrial Establishments Act is contained in *A.R.Q.D.L.*, 1896.
19. *A.R.Q.D.L.*, 1897, p. 41.
20. Canada, *Labour Gazette*, 1901, pp. 1-2, 243, 318, 370, 422, 488, 554.
21. By 1900 all Montreal Catholic Schools were graded "excellent" in all categories by the school inspector. See *Report of the Superintendent of Public Instruction, School Inspectors Reports 1900*.
22. Elzéar Pelletier. "Memoir on School Hygiene," *A.R.Q.B.H.*, 1900, p. 25.
23. M. C. Urquhart and K. Buckley, eds., *Historical Statistics of Canada* (Toronto, 1965), p. 595.
24. *Ibid.*, p. 593.
25. *Report of the Superintendent of Public Instruction*, 1901, p. xxiii.
26. *Ibid.*, 1897, p. 383.
27. John Spargo, *The Bitter Cry of the Children* (New York, 1903).
28. See Suzanne Cross, "The Neglected Majority: The Changing Role of Women in 19th Century Montreal." *Histoire social/Social History*, VI, Nov., 1973, pp. 202-23.

2 The Real Incomes of the Working Class

1. See *Labour Gazette* 1910-1929 for monthly budget prices.
2. Phyllis Heaton, "Standard of Living Studies" (Unpublished M.A. thesis, McGill University, 1935).
3. *Ibid.*
4. My calculations, Census of 1901, Vol. III, Manufacturing, pp. 232-36.
5. Urquhart and Buckley, *op. cit.*, p. 303.
6. Census of 1901, Vol. III, p. xiii.
7. My calculations, Census of 1911, Vol. III, pp. 76-81, 306-9.
8. Census of 1921, Vol. III, p. xx.
9. *Souvenir Handbook, Child Welfare Exhibit*, Montreal 1912, p. 32.
10. *Ibid.*, p. 33.
11. *Ibid.*, p. 32.
12. Canada, *Report of the Royal Commission to inquire into Industrial Disputes in the Cotton Factories of the Province of Quebec*, Sessional Paper 39, 1909.
13. *A.R.Q.D.L.*, 1915, p. 71.
14. The Montreal Trades and Labour Council reported unemployment reached 23 per cent in 1914. *Labour Gazette*, March 1914, p. 1026.
15. Department of Labour, *Wages and Hours of Labour in Canada 1900-1920*, Supplement to the *Labour Gazette*, March 1921.
16. *A.R.Q.D.L.*, 1916, p. 109.
17. *Labour Gazette*. November 1921, p. 1399.
18. L. C. Marsh. *Employment Research*. McGill Social Research Series #1, 1933, p. 142.
19. My calculations, Census of 1921, Vol. III, pp. 248-64.
20. *Ibid.*, Vol. III, p. xix.
21. My calculations, Census of 1921, Vol. III, pp. 248-64.
22. My calculations, Census of 1921, Vol. III, p. xviii.
23. *Labour Gazette* 1922, p. 518.
24. *Ibid.*, p. 965.
25. *Ibid.*, p. 518
26. *Ibid.*, 1924, p. 480.
27. Marsh, *op. cit.*, p. 265.

28. Urquhart and Buckley, *op. cit.*, p. 84.
29. Department of Labour, *Wages and Hours of Labour in Canada* 1920-1929, Supplement to the *Labour Gazette*, 1929.
30. Marsh, *op. cit.*, p. 261.
31. L. C. Marsh. *Canadians In and Out of Work*, McGill Social Research Series #9, 1940, p. 182.
32. As indicated in the text, changes in Marsh's original figures *Ibid.*, p. 183 were made with unemployment adjustments based on Marsh, *Employment Research,* Table XIIa, "Incidence of Unemployment and Lost Time: Wage Earners in Montreal 1930-31 (Males)" p. 264. Proportions of the labour force are from *Ibid.*, Table 22 (b), p. 316. The totals do not equal 100 because of "other and unspecified workers." Marsh included a non-monetary income estimate for service workers which has been omitted here.
33. Marsh, *Canadians, op. cit.*, p. 194.
34. *Ibid.*, p. 183.
35. *Ibid.*, p. 199.
36. *Ibid.*, p. 154-59.
37. Canada, *Board of Inquiry into Cost of Living*, 1915, Vol. I, pp. 522-24.

3 Women and Children in the Labour Force

1. Ames, *op. cit.*, p. 36.
2. Census of 1921, Vol. III, p. 264.
3. Census of 1931, Vol. VII, p. 190.
4. Census of 1921, Vol. III, p. 264-74.
5. Text of Industrial Establishments Act.
6. *A.R.Q.D.L.*, 1920, p. 67.
7. This agreement was however honoured more in the breach than in the observance. See the reports in the *Labour Gazette*, 1924, p. 243 for original agreement and the summary of "Strikes and Lockouts" for 1925 in the *Labour Gazette,* 1926, p. 96.
8. Department of Labour, *Hours of Labour in Canada*, Report No. 9, Supplement to the *Labour Gazette*, 1926.
9. *A.R.Q.D.L.*, 1919, p. 67.
10. *Ibid.*, 1928, p. 128.
11. *Ibid.*, 1928, pp. 137-38.
12. *Ibid.*, 1929, p. 55.
13. *Ibid.*, 1930, p. 71.
14. *Ibid.*, 1930, p. 73.
15. *Ibid.*, 1897, p. 67
16. *Ibid.*, 1903, p. 177.
17. *Ibid.*, 1905, p. 191.
18. *Ibid.*, 1905, p. 186.
19. *Ibid.*, 1922, p. 87-88.
20. John Spargo, *The Bitter Cry of the Children (Chicago, 1968), p. 148.*
21. Ames, *op. cit.*, p. 36.
22. Spargo, *op. cit.*, p. 145.
23. *A.R.Q.D.L.*, 1897, p. 41.
24. *Ibid.*, 1901, p. 160.
25. *Ibid.*, 1901, p. 170.
26. *Ibid.*, 1905, p. 192.
27. *Ibid.*, 1907, p. 107.
28. *Ibid.*, 1905, p. 186.

29. *Ibid.*, 1898, p. 64.
30. *Ibid.*, 1903, p. 192.
31. *Ibid.*, 1903, p. 193.
32. *Ibid.*, 1912, p. 173.
33. *Ibid.*, 1897, p. 64.
34. *Ibid.*, 1903, p. 193.
35. *Ibid.*, 1903, p. 193.
36. *Ibid.*, 1910, p. 76.
37. *Ibid.*, 1910, p. 79.
38. *Ibid.*, 1913, p. 63.
39. *Ibid.*, 1920, p. 73.
40. *Ibid.*, 1920, p. 74.
41. *Ibid.*, 1916, p. 57.
42. *Ibid.*, 1918, p. 69.
43. *Ibid.*, 1922, p. 86.
44. *Ibid.*, 1922, p. 80.
45. *Ibid.*, 1922-29.
46. *Ibid.*, 1925, p. 67.
47. *Ibid.*, 1927, p. 75.
48. Calculated from Census of 1921, Vol. IV, Table 5.
49. *A.R.Q.D.L.*, 1911, p. 5.
50. *Ibid.*, 1930, p. 58.
51. *Ibid.*, 1921, p. 67.
52. *Ibid.*, 1905, p. 230.
53. *Ibid.*, 1909, p. 100.
54. See Canada, Department of Labour, *The Employment of Children and Young Persons in Canada,* December 1930.

4 Formal Education and the Working Class

1. Supporters of the existing system of education always argued that Quebec's system resulted in better school attendance than in the other provinces. Professor Levitt in his admirable study of the social programme of the Quebec Nationalists, *Henri Bourassa and the Golden Calf* (Ottawa, 1969), points out that Bourassa "saw no virtue in the spread of mass education," but recognizes that this was not a general view. It might be well for me to state flatly that the role of the *nationalistes* in the debates over education and indeed the other questions dealt with in this study seems to me to have been of minor importance. The approach of Bourassa, Fournier and Heroux was, to put it politely, highly theoretical. Lavergne need not be considered at all. Olivar Asselin, on the other hand, was frequently well informed and relatively concrete in his approach to education and other issues.
2. *A.R.S.P.I.*, 1900-1929, Statistics of Roman Catholic Classical Colleges.
3. Cited in Levitt, *op. cit.*, p. 85.
4. The curriculums of the Protestant and Catholic primary schools are outlined in the Report of the Superintendent of Public Instruction, 1897 and 1898.
5. See Leonard C. Marsh, *Canadians In and Out of Work,* 1940, *Op. Cit.*, especially Chapter Seven, for an analysis of the ethnic composition of various components of the labour force in 1931. He observes that "the outstanding feature of the clerical class in Canada is the large proportion of British born," p. 151, and that "Neither English-Canadians nor French-Canadians match this weight (of British born) within the skilled ranks, their quota being more or less equal at a little less than the general average," p. 156.

6. The most obvious reference would be to the writings of Errol Bouchette (see *L'Indépendance économique du Canada français*, Montreal, 1913) but the need for technical education was stressed by almost everyone interested in education. See, for example, *Le Canada*, March 16, 1908.

7. Michel Brunet, *Québec, Canada Anglais* (Montreal, 1968), pp. 87-88.

8. The pages of *Le Canada* and, after 1910, *Le Pays* are the best source for a running account of Langlois' battle for educational reform. Langlois was interested in a wide range of reform issues and identified strongly with contemporary American progressive movements. *Le Canada* was "un organe du Parti Libéral" but its loyalties were to Laurier. On provincial and municipal political issues the newspaper reflected the independent *rouge* views of Langlois who was its editor until 1910. After 1910, Langlois edited *Le Pays* where he allowed himself the luxury of an editorial style that won interdiction of the paper from Archbishop Bruchési. Langlois accepted an appointment as Quebec representative in Brussels in 1914 and left the country in disgust. The leadership of the compulsory education movement passed for a time to Dr. J. T. Finnie, then to T. D. Bouchard who carried on Langlois' iconoclastic rougeism through another generation. I have been forced to modify my earlier admiration for Langlois because of the realization that his tactics were counter-productive but others might find the study of his career of great interest.

10. For a good summary of the polemical debate, see Jean-Claude Charbonneau, "The Lay School Movement in Quebec since 1840" (Unpublished M.A. thesis, McGill University 1971).

11. The recommendations of the 1909 Royal Commission on the Catholic Public Schools of Montreal (See Sessional Paper No. 68, 1911) for amalgamation of the various school boards were not immediately implemented but school consolidation proceeded rapidly after 1915. See Arthur Tremblay, "Le Système Scolaire" in Jean-Claude Falardeau, ed., *Essais Sur Le Québec Contemporain* (Quebec City, 1953).

12. Robert Rumilly, *Histoire de la Province de Québec* (Montreal, 1930), Vol. XII, p. 90.

13. *A.R.S.P.I.*, 1905-06, p. 386.

14. Provincial Association of Protestant Teachers, *Report of the School Attendance Committee* (Montreal, 1918).

15. *Ibid.*, p. 11

16. See "Extract of School Laws" in M.C.S.C., *Sketch of the Schools of Montreal* (Montreal, 1915).

17. *A.R.S.P.I.*, 1905-06, pp. 378-91.

18. Kindergartens were established in Protestant schools in 1892. No such facility was developed in the Catholic public schools though large numbers of five-year olds were accommodated in ordinary classrooms, swelling the registration figures for the first grade.

19. *Sketch of the Schools of Montreal, op. cit.*

20. *A.R.S.P.I.*, 1899-1900, pp. 332-33.

21. *Ibid.*, 1903-04, p. 341.

22. *Ibid.*, 1905-06, p. 343.

23. P.S.C.M., *Annual Report,* 1907-08, p. 8.

24. *Ibid.*, 1907-08, p. 19.

25. *Ibid.*, 1929, p. 19

26. *Ibid.*, 1916, p. 16.

27. Cited in *Report of the School Attendance Committee, op. cit.*, p. 14.

28. M.C.S.C., *Financial Report 1926-27*, p. 7.

29. Tremblay, *op. cit.*, p. 173.

30. René Fandrich, *L'École Primaire Supérieure* (Montreal, 1934), p. 43.

31. P.S.C.M., *The Financial Conditions and Needs of the Protestant Schools of Montreal* (Montreal, 1908).
32. P.S.C.M., *Annual Reports,* 1908-1929.
33. Montreal, *Annual Report of the City Treasurer,* 1919-1929.
34. Figure calculated by dividing school enrolment into municipal tax grants.
35. It is not possible to calculate the expenditures of classical colleges and other private schools from published statistics.
36. See F. C. Ensign, *Compulsory School Attendance and Child Labour* (New York, 1921), for an account of the struggle to adopt and enforce compulsory attendance laws in the United States. Ensign makes it clear that their legislation did not mean enforcement and many state laws remained dead letters up to 1921.

5 Housing Conditions

1. *Le Canada,* February 11, 1904.
2. Canada, *Board of Inquiry Into the Cost of Living* (Ottawa, 1913), p. 483.
3. B. J. Newman, "Housing Evils and Their Causes," *Addresses Delivered Before the Canadian Club of Montreal,* 1912-13, p. 157.
4. *A.R.M.B.H.* 1919, p. 27.
5. *Ibid.*, 1921, p. 60.
6. Percy A. Robert, "Dufferin District," (Unpublished M.A. Thesis, McGill University, 1928).
7. *A.R.Q.B.H.* 1908-09, p. 10.
8. *Ibid.,* 1909-10, p. 58.
9. Mary H. Davidson, "The Social Adjustment of British Immigrant Families in Verdun and Point St. Charles" (Unpublished M.A. Thesis, McGill University, 1933), p. 18.
10. Arthur St. Pierre, *Le Problème Social,* (Montreal, 1926) p. 101.
11. The data in this paragraph is drawn from the Reports of the Sanitary Inspectors in *A.R.M.B.H.,* 1901-1929.
12. See *A.R.Q.B.H.,* 1901-02 for an abridged version of the Act.
13. *A.R.Q.B.H.* 1908-09, p. 10
14. *Ibid.,* 1908-09, p. 19.
15. *Ibid.,* 1908-09, p. 58.
16. *Ibid.,* 1908-09, p. 58.
17. *A.R.M.B.H.* 1911, p. 4. The placard read "This room may not be occupied."
18. *Ibid.,* 1916, p. 34.
19. *Ibid.,* 1916, p. 34.
20. *Ibid.,* 1927, p. 46.
21. *Ibid.,* 1927, p. 34.
22. *Ibid.,* 1925, p. 46.
23. *Ibid.,* 1929, p. 118-20.
24. Lawrence Vellier, *Housing Reform,* (New York, 1910), p. 89.
25. *Ibid.,* pp. 20-81.
26. *Ibid.,* p. 83.
27. The platform is printed in Alfred Charpentier, "Le Mouvement Politique Ouvrier de Montréal 1883-1929," *Relations Industrielles,* Vol. 10 (1956), pp. 74-95.
28. L'Abbé E.E.M. Gouin, "Le Logement de la Famille Ouvrière," *L'École Sociale Populaire,* No. 9 (Montreal, 1912), p. 12.
29. Ontario, *Report of the Ontario Housing Committee* (Toronto, 1919), p. 43.
30. This discussion of Federal and Provincial housing policy is based on St. Pierre, *Le Problème Social, op. cit.* pp. 119-24.

31. Vellier, *op. cit.,* p. 89.
32. Charter of the City of Montreal, 62 Vict., Ch. 58, 1899, Corrected and Compiled Edition with all Amendments Adopted up to date 1908 (Montreal, 1908).
33. Montreal, *Amendments to the Charter, 1909* (Montreal, 1909).
34. Montreal, *Amendments to the Charter, 1924* (Montreal 1924).
35. St. Pierre, *Le Problème Social, op. cit.* pp. 99-100.
36. *Annual Report of the City Improvement League,* 1909, p. 7. Cited in William Baird, "The City Improvement League of Montreal" (Unpublished B.A. Honours Essay, Loyola College, 1970).
37. *Ibid.,* pp. 15-20.
38. *An Act to Establish the Metropolitan Parks Commission,* published as an appendix to the *Annual Report of the City Improvement League,* 1912.
39. Walter Vaughan, *The Life and Work of Sir William Van Horne* (New York, 1920), pp. 343-45.
40. *Souvenir Handbook of the Child Welfare Exhibit,* 1912, p. 29.
41. *Ibid.,* p. 30.

6 Public Health

1. See Fraser Brockington, *A Short History of Public Health* (London, 1966), for a survey of British public health practices.
2. See R. D. Defries, ed., *The Development of Public Health in Canada,* (Toronto, 1940), for a brief review of the history of public health legislation in each province.
3. *A.R.Q.B.H.,* 1903-04, p. 60
4. *Ibid.*
5. Quebec, *Royal Commission on Health and Social Welfare* (The Castonguay-Neveau Report), 1966, Vol. I, p. 29.
6. Montreal Health Survey Committee, *Survey of Public Health Activities,* (Montreal, 1928), Chapter XXII, Laboratory Service.
7. British Medical Association, *Souvenir of Montreal 1897,* p. 143.
8. See map of "Health Activities," Montreal Health Survey, *op. cit.* p. 17.
9. The public health by-laws introduced in 1901 and 1906 are included in *A.R.Q.B.H.* for those years.
10. *A.R.M.B.H.,* 1916, p. 46.
11. J. G. Fitzgerald, *An Introduction to the Practice of Preventive Medicine* (St. Louis 1926), p. 539. Fitzgerald was the Director of the School of Hygiene and the Connaught Labratories, University of Toronto.
12. Cited in *Ibid.,* p. 540-41.
13. Quebec Board of Health, *Bulletin Sanitaire,* 1926.
14. See Dr. Séverin Lachapelle's *Manuel d'Hygiène* (Montreal, 1890), *La Santé pour tous* (Montreal, 1890), and *Femme et nurse* (Ottawa, 1901).
15. *Bulletin Sanitaire,* 1926, p. 155.
16. This information on pasteurization was "confirmed" in an interview with a gentleman long active in the city's dairy industry who had better remain anonymous. The interview was not a particularly harmonious encounter.
17. J. C. Harrison, *The Milk Supply of Montreal* (Ottawa, 1914), p. 13.
18. *Ibid.,* p. 33.
19. *Ibid.,* p. 67.
20. For example in 1907 *Le Canada* published a series of articles around the theme *Le lait qui tue.*
21. *A.R.M.B.H.,* 1912, p. 12.
22. *Ibid.,* 1912, pp. 12-18.
23. *Ibid.,* 1916, p. 48.

24. *Ibid.*, 1916, p. 48.
25. *Ibid.*, 1928, p. 44.
26. *Ibid.*, 1926, p. 118a.
27. *Ibid.*, 1927, pp. 28-57.
28. *Montreal Health Survey*, p. 62.
29. See Appendix, Quebec, *Royal Commission on Tuberculosis* (Quebec, 1909).
30. Quebec, *Royal Commission on Tuberculosis*, p. 121.
31. `Ibid.*, pp. 7-9.
32. *A.R.M.B.H.*, 1921, p. 41.
33. *Ibid.*, 1924, p. 43.
34. *Ibid.*, 1924, p. 44.
35. *Montreal Health Survey*, p. 70.
36. Fitzgerald, *op. cit.*, p. 97.
37. Based on *Ibid.*, Chapter II.
38. The Montreal Health Department began to distribute small amounts of free vaccine to families who could not pay for it in 1928. A doctor's certificate stating that the family was unable to pay was required. *A.R.M.B.H.*, 1928, p. 143.
39. *Montreal Health Survey*, p. 16.
40. *Ibid.*, p. 17.
41. *Ibid.*, p. 7.
42. *Ibid.*, 142-43.
43. *Ibid.*, p. 24.
44. *Ibid.*, p. 25.
45. *A.R.M.B.H.*, 1927-1939.

7 Welfare

1. M.C.O.S., *Annual Report*, 1902, Appendix.
2. Montreal, *Annual Report of the Recorders Court*, 1898, p. 34.
3. Quebec, *Statistical Yearbook*, 1915, pp. 384-93.
4. *Rapport du Conseil Supérieur du Canada de la Société St-Vincent de Paul* (Quebec, 1930).
5. Francis Maclean, "Effects Upon Private Charity of the Absence of All Public Relief," *Proceedings of the National Conference on Charities and Corrections* (Washington, 1901), p. 143.
6. *Ibid.*, p. 145.
7. *Ibid.*, p. 145.
8. Cited in Robert Bremer, *op. cit.*, p. 47.
9. The Meurling came under the control of the Municipal Assistance Department which was also responsible for committing children to industrial schools, burying destitute persons and controlling tag days. The Department also had the power to make grants to organizations giving assistance to destitute persons if funds were available. In the winter of 1914 when heavy unemployment hit the city, all of $90,000 was appropriated to be divided proportionately on the basis of the population's religious affiliation. The St. Vincent de Paul Society, The Charity Organization Society and the Baron de Hirsch Institute were the three distributing agencies. Montreal, *Annual Report, Department of Municipal Assistance*, 1914, p. 49.
10. Quebec, *Report of the Director of the Bureau of Public Charities*, 1924. A 10 per cent amusement tax was levied to raise money for the Public Charities Fund. The municipality kept half of the sum collected, the remainder was forwarded to Quebec. Per diem rates were established for hospitals, sanatoriums, asylums, orphanages, etc. and it was necessary for such institutions to make individual applications for each indigent person served. The province would

then pay one-third of the per diem cost and the municipality a further third of the rate. Lump sum grants could be made to "Maternity Hospitals, Creches, Foundling Homes and divers charitable organizations." Article 17 of the Act left the province free to help other institutions in "urgent cases." See Dorothy Aikin, "The Role of the Montreal Council of Social Agencies in the Establishment of Public Assistance" (Unpublished M.A. thesis, University of Chicago, 1950), for a discussion of the evolution of the Act.

For a detailed discussion of the controversy over the Act instigated by Henri Bourassa's pamphlet, *La Mauvaise Loi*, which attacked the legislation as an unacceptable intervention by the state in the area reserved to the church, see A. Dupont, "The Conflict of Church and State Under Tachereau" (Unpublished Ph.D. Thesis, McGill University, 1970). My own view is that the opposition of Bourassa and a few other ultramontane idealists was of little importance in view of the general support for the legislation. Bourassa's role does, of course, raise questions about his ideas and influence but that is another problem.

11. Quebec, *Annual Report, Inspector of Reformatories and Industrial Schools, Sessional Paper* #4, 1906, p. 131.
12. *Ibid.*, 1900, p. 143.
13. *Ibid.*, 1898, p. 130.
14. *Ibid.*, 1909-10, p. 17.
15. *Ibid.*, 1905, p. 168.
16. *Ibid.*, 1907-08, p. 147. The "Girls Cottage School," a home for girls, paralleling Shawbridge, was established in 1911.
17. See *Ibid.*, Reports on "Montfort Industrial School," 1897-1910.
18. M.C.O.S., 1901, p. 3.
19. *Ibid.*, p. 17.
20. *Ibid.*, p. 22.
21. *Ibid.*, p. 21.
22. *Ibid.*, 1903, passim.
23. *Ibid.*, 1905, passim.
24. *Ibid.*, 1906, p. 7.
25. Cited in Bremer, *op. cit.*, p. 54.
26. *Ibid.*, p. 55.
27. Allen F. Davis, *Spearheads of Reform* (New York, 1967), p. 21.
28. Allen Davis deals largely with the role of social settlement workers in neighbourhood activities and in agitating for reform legislation. Montreal had several social settlements but their organizers were not noted for their role as a pressure group for reform. It should be noted that Davis does not conclude that the settlement workers won great victories but rather that they spearheaded a reform movement.
29. M.C.O.S., 1912, p. 13.
30. *Ibid.*, 1919, p. 7.
31. *Ibid.*, 1919, p. 10.
32. *Ibid.*, 1920, p. 12.
33. Howard Toynbee Falk was born into a family of social workers. His father who had been active in German welfare organizations married a Toynbee. Howard Falk worked at Toynbee Hall as a young man and knew the Webbs and other Fabians. Upon immigrating to Canada he became a close friend of J. S. Woodsworth who encouraged him to prepare a survey of welfare activities in Winnipeg. Falk worked for the Red Cross during the war and served on the Halifax Disaster Committee. He arrived in Montreal in 1918 to become director of the new School of Social Work of McGill University. See W. C. Shepard, "The Genesis of the Montreal Council of Social Agencies" (Unpublished Master's Thesis, McGill School of Social Work, 1957).

34. *Report of a Committee of the Montreal Council of Social Agencies*, Montreal, 1919, p. 18.
35. *Ibid.*, p. 20.
36. Cited in Aikin, *op. cit.*, p. 61.
37. The Council argued that the Protestant community constituted 12.2 per cent of the population but received only 9.4 per cent of the institutional grants and 8.5 per cent of the special grants. *Ibid.*, p. 61.
38. Quebec, *Social Insurance Commission*, 1933, p. 48.
39. The creation of a juvenile court and probation system in Montreal was primarily the work of the Children's Aid Society which was formed in 1908 after the Montreal Women's Club had been drawn into W. C. Scott's campaign for the passage of a Juvenile Delinquents Act by the Dominion Parliament. Scott, an Ottawa social worker, had drafted a bill which got around the problems of Federal-Provincial Jurisdiction by defining delinquency as an "act" subject to the criminal code rather than a "condition" which would place delinquency within provincial jurisdiction. In the early stages there was strong support in Montreal from members of both linguistic communities and the legislation was quickly introduced in the Senate by F. W. Beique, a close associate of Laurier and a leading French Canadian "progressive." Scott had argued from American and Ontario precedents; Beique reviewed European practices in his Senate speech. The bill went to the Commons where it was accepted without comment. The legislation was potentially controversial for it allowed the Federal Government to set up courts if a province failed to do so. The Quebec legislature created a court for Montreal in 1912, but no appropriation for probation officers was made. The Children's Aid Society was able to fund a partial probation service for Protestants but no system was developed for Catholics.

    For a general account, see L. G. Mendelsohn and S. Ronald, "History of the Montreal Juvenile Court" (Unpublished Master's Thesis, McGill School of Social Work, 1969). The Senate debate occurred on May 21, 1908. Canada *Senate Debates*, 1908, p. 1045.
40. *A. R.Q.D.L.* 1897-98, p. 64.
41. *Ibid.*, p. 64.
42. *Ibid.*, p. 60.
43. *Ibid.*, 1900-01, p. 120-21.
44. Quebec, *Report of the Commission on Labour Accidents* (Quebec City, 1907), p. 17.
45. *Ibid.*, p. 11.
46. Guyon attended the conferences as the Quebec Government's delegate. For his report see *A. R.Q.D.L.* 1900-01, p. 165.
47. *Ibid.*, 1909-10, p. 76.
48. *Commission on Labour Accidents,, op. cit.*, p. 5.
49. *Ibid.*, p. 6.
50. For a brief discussion of the Ontario Act and the opposition to it see J. Castell Hopkins, *The Canadian Annual Review* (Toronto, 1914)
51. Quebec, *Report of the Investigation Commission on Compensation in Labour Accidents, Sessional Papers*, Vol. I, 1925.
52. See *Labour Gazette* 1922, p. 3, 1924, p. 204, 1926, p. 662 for examples of this opposition on the past of the Quebec branch of the Canadian Manufacturers Association.
53. *Labour Gazette*, 1926, p. 324.
54. See Robert F. Wesser, "Conflict and Compromise: The Workmen's Compensation Movement in New York 1890's-1913," *Labour History*, Vol. 12, No. 3, 1971, pp. 345-72, for an account of similar employer opposition in New York State.

55. David N. Noble, *The Progressive Mind*, 1890-1917 (Chicago, 1970), p. viii.

8 Labour Unrest and Industrial Conflict

1. Stuart Jameson, *Times of Trouble: Labour Unrest and Industrial Conflict in Canada, 1900-1966* (Ottawa, 1968), p. 23.
2. *Ibid.*, p. 39.
3. Michael Piva, a graduate student at Sir George Williams University, compiled the information on strikes in Montreal reported in the *Labour Gazette* for this study. All of the information on labour unrest in Montreal not otherwise cited is taken from this compilation except statements on wages and hours which are from *Wages and Hours of Labour in Canada 1901-1920, Labour Gazette*, 1921 (Supplement) and subsequent bulletins, 1921-1929.
4. Canada, *Report of the Royal Commission to Inquire into Industrial Disputes in the Cotton Factories of the Province of Quebec* (Ottawa, 1909).
5. *A.R.Q.D.L.*, 1915, p. 71.
6. *Montreal Gazette*, Dec. 2, 1918.
7. *Ibid.*, Dec. 14, 1918.
8. *Canadian Annual Review*, 1918, p. 336.
9. *A.R.Q.D.L.*, 1921, p. 136.
10. *Ibid.*, 1916, p. 109.
11. *Ibid.*, 1919-1920, p. 143.
12. *Ibid.*, 1919-1920, p. 149-51.
13. *Ibid.*, 1921, p. 86.
14. *Documentary History of the Amalgamated Clothing Workers* 1926-1928 (Cincinnati, 1928), p. 48.
15. *Ibid.*, p. 167.
16. This account of the *Parti Ouvrier* is based largely on information summarized in Alfred Charpentier, "Le Mouvement Politique Ouvrier de Montréal (1883-1929)," *Relations Industrielles*, Vol. 10 (1956) pp. 74-95.

9 Conclusion

1. Leonard C. Marsh, "The Problem of Seasonal Unemployment" (Unpublished typescript, Research Project No. 22, McGill Social Research Series, 1933), p. 100.
2. Marsh, *Employment Research, op. cit.*, Appendix A, Tables 9A, 9B.
3. Marsh, "Seasonal Unemployment," *op. cit.*, Statistical Tables, pp. 161-72.
4. The best known argument supporting the view that the key variable in the industrial development of Quebec and Ontario was entrepreneurship is Norman Taylor, "The French Canadian Industrial Entrepreneur and His Social Environment," in Rioux and Martin, *French Canadian Society, Vol. I* (Carleton Library No. 18, Toronto, 1964). Whatever merit this argument has for Quebec as a whole its relevance for Montreal is very slight.
5. "Shipping," the D.B.S. category for employment related to the harbour, provided jobs for 8.3 per cent of the non-manufacturing labour force in Montreal versus 0.4 per cent for Toronto. Marsh, "Seasonal Unemployment," *op. cit.*, p. 174.
6. A. Faucher and M. Lamontagne, "History of Industrial Development," in Jean C. Falardeau, ed., *Essais sur le Québec Contemporain* (Quebec City, 1953), p. 34.
7. Census of 1921, Vol. III, p. XXV.
8. *Ibid.*, p. XXV.

9. *Ibid.*, p. xxv.
10. *Ibid.*, p. xxv.
11. Huet Massue, "Graphic Review of Public Debt Revenues and Expenses of the Dominion of Canada and of the Provinces of Ontario and Quebec 1914-1937" (Montreal 1940, Unpublished typescript, McLennan Library, McGill University, Exhibits 13, 14).
12. *Ibid.*, Exhibits 11, 12.
13. *Ibid.*, Exhibit 17.
14. *Ibid.*, Exhibit 17, notes
15. Huet Massue, "Financial and Economic Situation of Montreal Compared with That of Toronto" (Montreal 1940, Unpublished typescript, McLennan Library, N.P. McGill University, Chart number 5).
16. *Ibid.*, Chart number 6.
17. *Ibid.*, Chart number 1.
18. *Ibid.*, Chart number 1.
19. *Ibid.*, Chart number 6.
20. See Michael Gauvin, "The Municipal Reform Movement in Montreal 1896-1914." (Unpublished M.A. thesis, University of Ottawa, 1972).
21. Municipal politics in Montreal did involve "real problems" in the sense that aldermen were important as dispensers of patronage and as intermediaries with police courts and for offices. Voter turnout was high (over 60 per cent) and aldermanic elections fiercely contested. Upper class groups were repelled by this type of politics but the alternatives offered by their short-lived reform movements were far too abstract to be of interest to the mass of the population.

Index

Addams, Jane, 118
agriculture, Quebec, 143
Ainey, Joseph, 138
Amalgamated Clothing Workers, 44; campaign to organize clothing industry, 135-36
American Civic Federation, 85
American Public Health Association, 92, 104
Ames, Herbert Brown, 18, 19, 21, 22, 23, 25, 26, 29, 44, 50, 70, 73, 80, 82, 84, 88
Andover Settlement House, 19
Angus, R. B., 118
Assistance Maternelle, 122
Atholstan, Lord, 101

Barry, Miss R., 53
Beecher, Henry Ward, 19
Blackadder, Dr. A. D., 99
Board of Control system, Montreal, 146
Board of Inquiry into the Cost of Living (1914), 70
Borden Government, 82
Boston, Mass., 19, 25
Boucher, Dr. S., 101
Bourassa, Henri, 138
Bremner, Robert H., 118
British Columbia: labour movement; 139, labour unrest, 137; legislation for women, 45
British Independent Labour Party, 137
British Public Health Act (1875), 88
Brothers of Charity, 112
Bruchési, Archbishop, 133
Bruchési Institute, 101
Brunet, Michel, 59, 60
Builder's Exchange, 125
Bulletin Sanitaire (of the Quebec Board of Health), 92, 96
Bureau of Labor Statistics (U.S.), 32

Canadian Brotherhood of Railway Employees, 32
Canadian Manufacturers' Association, 38, 125

Canadian Welfare Council, 40
Catholic School Board. *See* Montreal Catholic School Board
Catholic School Commissions, 62, 66
Catholic syndicates, 123
Census of 1901: data on employment and income, 32; information on child labour, 50
Census of 1911, data on employment and income, 32
Census of 1921: data on employment and income, 30, 35, 36, 38; data on women in labour force, 44
Census of 1931: data on children in labour force, 56; data on employment and income, 30, 35, 39; data on women in labour force, 44
Charitable agencies and institutions: Anglo-Protestant, 121, 126-27; Catholic, 126; private, 109. *See also* Bureau of Public Charity, *Directory of some Montreal Charities*, Montreal Charity Organization Society, Welfare
Charity Organization Society. *See* Montreal Charity Organization Society
Chicago, Ill., 23, 109
Child Welfare Exhibition, Montreal 1912, 34, 37
Children in labour force: as apprentices, 56; attitudes toward, 51; crusade for abolition of child labour, 50-51; education of, 52, 53; exceptions to child labour law, 52; income of, 32-33; legislation restricting certain occupations to, 45; in part time jobs, 29; role in work force, specific to Montreal, 50; solutions to problem in countries other than Canada, 53
Christian Brothers, 63
C.I.L. *See* Montreal City Improvement League
City and Suburban Homes Association," 23
"City Below the Hill" (Ames), 15, 50
City Improvement Plan, 86

Coats, R. H., 43
Cochrane, Mayor, 130
Confédération des travailleurs catholiques du Canada, 136-37
Confessions of a Reformer (Howe), 117
Council of Public Instruction, 60
Currie, Sir Arthur, 101

Davis, Allen F., 118
Department of Labor (U.S.), 31
Department of Labour: family budget, 31, 32, 35; index numbers for weekly wages, 34; surveys of Hours of Labour in Canada, 39, 45; survey of trade unions, 28
Depression, Great, 105, 148
Diamond Court, 23
Diphtheria, 26, 88, 92, 103. *See also* Schick test
Directory of some Montreal Charities (1901), 106
Dominion Textile Company, 34, 131, 134
Dominique, Brother, 112
Drummond, George, 118
Drummond, Lady, 119
Dufferin Square, 18, 73

École des Hautes Études Commerciales, 58, 60
École St.-Louis, 68
L'École Sociale Populaire, 81
Education: Catholic, 58; conditions in 1890s, 28-29; French Canadian compared with English Canadian, 58-59; opportunities for available to working-class children, 57; position of foreign children in Montreal's school system, 67; proposals for compulsory, 53-54; public education system, 62-63; secularization of, 67; Protestant, 58; state, 58
Ely, Robert E., 19
Employment Research (March), 35
L'Enseignement Primaire, 60

Factories, health conditions in, 48
Falk, John Howard Toynbee, 120-21, 122
Falk Report, 120-21
Family Welfare Association, 31

Fathers of the Society of St. Mary, 114
Faucher, Albert, 143-44
Federal Old Age Pensions Act (1927), 123
Fédération Nationale, 123
Financial Conditions and Needs of the Protestant Schools of Montreal, The (1908), 68
Fitzgerald, Dr. J. G., 102
Forget, L. J., 118, 130
Francq, Gustave, 47, 138

Gouin, L'Abbé E.E.M., 81-82
Gouin, Lomer, 60, 126, 133, 138, 145
"Gouttes de Lait," 98, 99
Great Depression. *See* Depression
Greek Orthodox Church, 67
Griffintown, 25
Guyon, Louis, 27, 49- 49-50, 51, 52, 53, 54-55, 123, 124-25

harbour, effect on employment, 143
Hilduard, Brother, 112-13
Hochelaga riding, 138
Hours of Labour in Canada, 39, 45
Housing: absentee landlords, 70; crisis during World War I, 71; dark rooms, 71, 75, 76, 119; described in "City Below the Hill," 17; development of loan funds for, 82; sanitary conditions, 23-24, 27, 71, 73-74, 75, 76, 77, 79, 83, 119; shortage of during 1904, 70
Housing Reform (Vellier), 80
Howe, Frederic C., 117

Illiteracy, 53, 54
Independent Labour Party, 138
Industrial Establishments Act (I.E.A.), (1893), 26, 51, 53, 55, 56
Industrialization, influence of cultural environment upon, 144
Industrial schools. See Reformatories and industrial schools
Industries, major Montreal, 21
Infant Hygienic Division, Municipal Health Department, 99
Infant mortality: in England and Wales, 93; higher rate among French Canadians, 95; from influences in post-natal environment, 93, 96; milk supply as key factor in, 96-97; rate, 1899-1901, 25-26; rate, 1927, 100; rate, by ethnic group, 95; rate, of

illegitimate children, 95; "Safety Zone" defined by U.S. Department of Labor, Children's Bureau, 93, 95

International Convention on Accident and Social Insurance (Fifth), 124

International Ladies Garment Workers Union, 135

Jameson, Stuart, 128, 129, 137

Jewish immigration to Montreal, 67

Jews, legal right to attend Protestant schools, 67

Juvenile courts, 123

Kelso, J. J., 122

King, Louisa, 48-49, 51

King, Mackenzie, 131

Knights of Labour, 27

Koch, Robert, 89

Laberge, Dr. Louis, 91

Labour Gazette, 129, 130, 132, 135

Lachapelle, Dr. E. P., 92

Lachapelle, Dr. Séverin, 96, 99

Lafontaine Park, 18

Lamontagne, Maurice, 143-44

Lane, Robert H., 117

Langlois, Godfroy, 59, 60

Laval University Medical Faculty, 89, 99

League of American Municipalities, 85

Lighthall, W. D., 86

Ligue de l'Enseignement, 59, 60

Loi des Habitations Salubres (1919), 83

Lowell, Josephine Shaw, 110, 116

Maclean, Francis, 109, 115, 117

Maisonneuve, 138

Manitoba, 139

Marchand Academy, 68

Marchand, Felix-Gabriel, 28

Marois, Felix, 134

Marsh, Leonard C., 35, 39, 40

Martin, Mayor Medéric, 138, 147

McGill University Medical Faculty, 89, 99

"Memoir on the Division of the School Tax in Montreal," 63-66

Metropolitan Parks Commission, 86

Meurling Refuge, 109-10

Milk control, 104. *See also* "Gouttes de Lait," Infant mortality, Pasteurization

Minimum age, 51-52, 53. *See also* Children in Labour Force, Industrial Establishments Act

Ministry of Education, 59, 69

Ministry of Public Instruction, 28

Mitchell, James, 56

"Model tenement," 21, 22, 80, 85

Le Monde Ouvrier, 138

Montfort Agricultural Colony, 114

Montreal Anti-Tuberculosis and General Health League, 101, 103

Montreal Board of Health. *See* Montreal Department of Health

Montreal Catholic School Commission: comparisons with Protestant Central School Board, 69; endowments, 63; enrolment figures, 60-61; financial problems, 69; Financial Report for 1926-1927, 67; share of tax dollar, 68

Montreal Charity Organization Society, 108, 109; aims of, 115-20

Montreal City Improvement League (C.I.L.), 85-86

Montreal Council of Social Agencies, 120, 121, 122, 123

Montreal Council of Women, 121

Montreal Department of Health 9, 17, 76, 77, 91, 95, 102, 103, 104, 105, 144-45

Montreal Labour Bureau, 55

Montreal Protestant School Commission, 62

Montreal Technical Institute, 60

Montreal-Toronto, comparisons. *See* Toronto-Montreal, comparisons

Montreal, Wards cited in text: Delormier, 99; Hochelaga, 101; Laurier, 99; St. Andrew, 99, 100; St. Antoine, 25; St. Denis, 100; St. Gabriel, 25; St. George, 100; St. Henri, 17, 101; St. Jean Baptiste, 25; St. James, 25; St. Laurent, 18; St. Lawrence, 25; St. Mary's, 23; Ste. Anne's, 25, 100; Ste. Cunegonde, 17

Morals, protection of women's, 48. *See also* Provencher, Louise and King, Louisa

Mother's Allowance Acts, 123

Mothers Assistance Act (1937), 123

Mount Royal and Hampstead, 147

Mount Royal Park, 18

Municipal Board of Health. *See* Montreal Department of Health

Municipal Strike and Lockout Act
(1920), 133

National Conference of Charities and
Corrections (1901), 108
New Brunswick, 123
New York City: enrolment in schools,
61; infant mortality rate, 93, 97;
"model housing legislation," 80;
mortality rate 25, 26; tenements, 23.
See also Brooklyn
New York Association for Improving
the Conditions of the Poor, 23
Noble, David, 127
Normal Schools, 60

Olmstead, Frederick Law, 18, 86
Ontario: labour movement, 125, 139;
revenue and expenditure, compared
with Quebec, 145
Ontario Housing Accomodation Act
(1913), 82
"Organized Outdoor Relief"
(Maclean), 108
Ottawa, 61
"Our Unsanitary Dwellings"
(Pelletier), 76
Outremont, 147

Le Parti Ouvrier, 47, 81, 137-38
Pasteur, Louis, 89
Pasteurization, 97, 99, 100, 140
Pelletier, Elzéar, 18, 73, 75-76, 84, 92,
99
Pensions, old age, 123
Philadelphia Housing Commission, 71
Plateau Academy, 68
Playgrounds, 140
Point St. Charles, 116, 117
"Poverty: A Preventable Social
Waste," 119
La Presse, 137
Le Progrès Ouvrier, 138
Protestant Central School Board, 66,
67, 68
Protestant Committee of the Council of
Public Instruction, 63
Protestant ethic, 143
Protestant School Commission, *See*
Montreal Protestant School
Commission
Provencher, Louise, 48, 51,
56

Provincial Association of Protestant
Teachers, 61-62

Quebec Architects Association, 85
Quebec Board of Health, 18, 26, 28,
66, 75, 91, 92
Quebec Bureau of Public Charities, 111
Quebec City, strike by police and
firemen, 133
Quebec Commission on Labour
Accidents, 124, 125
Quebec Department of Labour, 35, 138
Quebec Public Charities Act (1921), 105
Quebec Public Health Act (1886), 75,
89, 91
Quebec Social Insurance Commission,
122
Quebec Statistical Yearbook, 129
Quebec Trade Disputes Act (1901), 134

Reformatories andindustrial schools,
112-14
Report of the Royal Commission on
Industrial Relations, 137
Richmond Square, 18
Rolland, J. D., 118
Royal Commission on Health and
Social Welfare, 91
Royal Commission on Industrial
Training and Technical Education
(1913), 58
Royal Commission on Tuberculosis
(1909), 100-1, 102
Royal Edward Institute, 100, 101
Russian Orthodox Church, 67

Sacré Coeur Hospital, 101
"Safety Museum," 124
St. George's Society, 108
St. Helen's Island, 18
St. Henri-Ste. Cunegonde-Westmount
area, 116
St. Martin, Albert, 138
St. Pierre, Arthur, 73, 84, 87, 122
St. Vincent de Paul Society, 107, 109,
111
Sherbrooke jail, 113
Schick test, 103
Sisters of Providence, 101
Smallpox epidemic of 1885-1886, 89
Smallpox vaccination, 26, 92

Spargo, John, 50
Strikes in Montreal, 1901-1927, 129-36

Taschereau, Louis Alexandre, 126, 145
Teamsters, 130
Textile industry, 29, 45, 47, 53-54, 56, 124, 141. *See also* Dominion Textile Company
Times of Trouble (Jameson), 129
Toronto Housing Company, 82
Toronto-Montreal, comparisons: age composition of family, 144; average family size, 144; average income, 140-41; average number of persons per family wholly supported by head of family, 144; definition of city limits, 147; economic benefits, 143; effectiveness of state in public health and housing, 144; enrolments, 61; industry, 141-42; infant mortality, 93; labour force, 141; mortality rate, 25; per capita expenditure and revenue, 146
Trade and Labour Council, 38, 123, 137, 138
Trade Union Educational League, 136
Tuberculosis, 88, 92, 100-1, 102-3, 104, 119
Typhoid fever, epidemic in Montreal, 99-100

Unmployment: data on, See Census of 1901, Census of 1911, Census of 1921, Census of 1931; opinions of by Montreal Charities Society, 119-20
Union of Canadian Municipalities, 85
Unions, 27-28, 29, 34, 35, 38, 43. *See also* Amalgamated Clothing Workers, Canadian Brotherhood of Railway Employees, International Ladies Garment Workers Union, Strikes, Teamsters, Trade and Labour Council, Trade Union Educational
United Textile Workers of America, 134

Van Horne, William, 86, 118
Vellier, Lawrence, 80-81, 83, 85
Verdun, 73

Verville, Alphonse, 138
Vickers Shipyards, 143
Viger Square, 18

Wages: incomes in "city below the hill," 21, 22; as related to productivity, 43; sex and age differentials, 1930-1931, 39; in various professions, 130-33. *See also* data on employment and income, Census of 1901, Census of 1911, Census of 1921, Census of 1931
War Measures Act, 82, 139
Welfare: Catholic, 106, 107, 121-22 (*see* also St. Vincent de Paul Society); education, 140; Jewish assistance to, 108; Protestant 107, 121-22 (*see also* St. George's Society); role of government in, 111-12; unique characteristics of Quebec's system, 106-7. *See also* Canadian Welfare Council, Charities, Child Welfare Exhibition, Family Welfare Association, Meurling Refuge, Royal Commission on Health and Social Welfare
Westmount, 147
Wheat boom, 130
White, Alfred T., 23
Women in labour force: attitudes, toward, 48-50; in domestic service, 44, 45; estimated percentage of all workers, 29; in factories and mills, 26, 33, 44, 45, 48; incomes, 32-33; legislation for and protection of, 45; statistics by job and age categories, 44-45. *See also* King, Louisa and Provencher, Madame Louise
Women's Minimum Wage Commission (1919), 45, 47, 48
Women's Minimum Wage Act, 55
Woods, Robert A., 19
Workman's Compensation Act (1909), 55, 124, 125
Workman's compensation, 123, 125, 126, 128
Work week, Ames' concept of, 26
World War I, 34, 132